THE
COST

THE COST

MY LIFE ON A TERRORIST HIT LIST

ALI HUSNAIN WITH J. CHESTER

ZONDERVAN

The Cost
Copyright © 2016 by Husnain Ali

Requests for information should be addressed to:
Zondervan, 3900 *Sparks Dr. SE, Grand Rapids, Michigan 49546*

Library of Congress Cataloging-in-Publication Data

Names: Husnain, Ali.
Title: The cost : my life on a terrorist hit list / Ali Husnain, with J. Chester.
Description: Grand Rapids : Zondervan, 2016.
Identifiers: LCCN 2015036830| ISBN 9780310344865 (hardcover) | ISBN 9780310344889
    (softcover) | ISBN 9780310344872 (ebook) | ISBN 9780310066545 (mobile app)
Subjects: LCSH: Husnain, Ali. | Christian biography—Pakistan. | Terrorism—Religious
    aspects—Christianity.
Classification: LCC BR1725.H857 A3 2016 | DDC 275.491/083092—dc23 LC record available
    at http://lccn.loc.gov/2015036830

Published in association with the literary agency of D.C. Jacobson and Associates LLC, an
Author Management Company, www.dcjacobson.com.

Cover design: Brian Bobel @ Dual Identity
Cover photo: © iStockphoto®
Interior design: Kait Lamphere

First printing January 2016 / Printed in the United States of America

To my aunt Gulshan,
for all your hard work and prayers

CONTENTS

ACKNOWLEDGMENTS

Thanks to Gordon and Rachel, Tim, Terry and Ann, Peter, and all the other people who have helped me over the years. You have been my brothers and sisters and I am more grateful than words can express.

Thank you to the wonderful team at Zondervan for being prepared to partner with me on this book.

IT WAS NEVER SUPPOSED TO END LIKE THIS

I had just turned seventeen, and nothing could have prepared me for how dangerous my life had become.

Three months had passed since the air had filled with angry shouts of *"Kafir!* Infidel!" and an army of hands of those I thought were my friends had forced me to the dusty ground, pinning me tight. Three months since I watched the black-robed *mullah* march up to me, a knife as long as my hand catching the late-afternoon sun. Three months since I felt the blade pierce my skin and drive deep between my ribs. Three months and still it hurt when I tried to use my left arm. Externally the only evidence of the stabbing was a thick scar as wide as my thumb, but the deep pain inside my chest was as fierce as ever. Still, it was nothing compared with the fear.

Being scarred was nothing compared with being scared.

My stomach remained permanently twisted, my breath constantly short, my muscles ready to send me running for cover at a moment's notice. In the weeks following that initial attack, as events unfolded and my life sank deeper and deeper into this suffocating quicksand I was in, the fear had only gotten worse. My appetite had decreased, what little sleep I'd been able to get before had all but vanished, and the ability to find within me a moment of stillness and calm had deserted me. All I'd been able to feel, all I'd been able to taste, all I'd been able to know, was fear.

In three months I had gone from being a confident young man who was starting to put his plan for his life into play, to this: a wounded boy who was afraid of the dark and desperate for his mother to come and take care of him. It wasn't a change in fortune that I'd been expecting. Anyone who knew me before the assault would have been shocked to see me in such a terrible state.

In Pakistan you can tell a lot about a person from their name. Family names carry great significance and are an instant way of revealing a person's breeding and social standing. And mine was about as prestigious as that of anyone I'd ever met.

My name is Ali Sayed Husnain Shah. It is a name conveying unmistakable high birth, with a family tree that stretches all the way back to the birth of Islam and Muhammad himself.

Ali is the name of the man who married Muhammad's first child and the very man who went on to be Muhammad's first-ever disciple and founder of the branch of Islam—Shia—to which my family belongs. People called Shah are also members of a highly respected caste, and Shahs are often found in the highest levels of society, from business to government.

But it is the name Sayed that really counts. We Sayeds are members of the highest caste in the land, attending the best universities, dispensing wisdom to our communities, and often living off the generosity of our disciples. Ours is a life of privilege, and privilege was the kind of life I had come to know. I was a young man on the rise, honored everywhere I went, whether the mosque or the country club. Yet none of that mattered now. Now I was living in a shack. A prince turned into an outcast.

My mother, Ami, hadn't visited me during the weeks I had spent in the shack. It was too dangerous. I understood that, but it hadn't stopped my tears, and I was always careful to muffle my crying with the solitary stained blanket I'd found beneath the bed.

But today, finally, I was leaving my little prison.

When Baba-jan, my stepfather, stepped carefully out of his dusty SUV, my little brother, Misim, ran toward me as if his life depended on it. For minutes we did not say anything; we just embraced at first and sat side by side, his little hand in mine, as silence stretched between us. It was the best kind of silence.

It did not take long for Baba-jan to gather up my possessions and load them into the car, and while he did, Misim and I sat in the car and took in the view. The building I'd been sleeping in for the last month was old and broken. Poorly fashioned bricks made up walls that looked as though they had been laid by an impatient child. The sheets of metal on the roof were rusted and choked with vines that reached out across the small clearing in the forest. With tall trees all around and too little sunlight filtering down, it looked more like a grave than the safe house it was meant to be.

I closed my eyes, waiting for Baba-jan to finish up inside the shack. "Nomi," said Misim, calling me by the nickname given to many a clever kid in Pakistan. Everyone had called me that when I was younger, and feeling Misim squeezing my hand gently as he spoke, I remembered what my life felt like before everything changed. "Baba-jan wanted to bring the Honda, but I told him to bring the Range Rover, see? I knew you'd like it better."

"That is good, Misim," I said, smiling and arching my back into the leather seats to show my appreciation. "Thank you." I looked at him. He had grown since I last saw him, and the first wisps of a mustache were appearing on his lip. His smile hadn't changed a bit, though. It was the same grin he wore whenever I took him to Uncle Faizal's arcade and gave him a handful of rupees to play video games, the same one that remained pasted all across his face whenever I let him ride on the front of my motorbike as we circled around the streets. But the smile vanished as soon as I spoke again. "Where is everyone else, Misim?" I wanted to see my sister, Zainab. I wanted to see Ami.

He looked away. "They are meeting us at the airport."

The drive there took an hour, maybe two. For the longest time we passed nothing but trees. All the time I had been in the shack, I knew that the forest was big, but it was only as we drove that I realized how truly vast it was. Mile after mile we shook along the track, nothing but trees on either side of us. "You see why you had to come here, Nomi?" said Baba-jan, catching my eye in the mirror. "It was the safest place for you."

Safe? I thought. *You have no idea what it was like.* I remembered the nights when every hour felt like a month. I remembered how I dreaded sunset and waited with increasing panic for the moment when the darkness outside took over and the sounds of the forest changed. Every night, I huddled, shivering and frightened, in the corner of the shack, wishing for the sun to rise and the noises to fade, trying my best to ignore the waking nightmare playing out in my mind. I'd whisper simple prayers under my breath, asking for help, protection, or even just a quick death that wouldn't hurt too much. Hour after hour I spent like this until the sun started to rise and the solitary window lightened enough to reveal the trees again. Only then would the adrenaline subside enough for me to crawl onto the *charpai*, the flimsy bed that supported a thin, stained mattress upon an even thinner web of ratty rope. Only when it was light could I finally try to sleep.

When at last we left the trees behind us and Baba-jan turned onto asphalt, I began to feel better. Misim started feeding me boiled sweets and soda, knowing I'd eaten little more than *dhal* and rice for the last month. He told me how good he was getting at cricket and why school continued to be terrible, but I didn't talk much. I wanted to ask him about Ami and Zainab, but I thought better of it. I didn't want him to have to lie again.

The combination of candy, Misim's occasional chatter, and the familiar comfort of the back seat of Baba-jan's car reminded me a little of what it felt like to be me again, the me I used to be before everything happened. I remembered what it felt like to drive my motorbike, how even with three of my friends packed onto it, the little 125cc engine managed to propel us along fast enough to leave a trail of chaos in the streets behind us.

I let myself start to picture what was coming next. I tried not to think too much about finally seeing Ami again; after ten weeks away from her, just thinking about our reunion was enough to fill my eyes with tears. Instead I remembered the plan as described to me by Baba-jan just a week earlier.

"You cannot stay here for the rest of your life," he'd said the last time he arrived at the shack with his weekly provisions. "It has been decided that you will go to England now." My face must have betrayed my panic, for he quickly added, "But not alone. You will go with your family; your mother, sister, and brother are all traveling with you."

It was a delicious thought, a proposition almost too wonderful to imagine. For the rest of that day, I allowed myself to soak in the idea of being reunited with the people I loved most. I daydreamed about returning to England and making a new start among the patchwork faces and gray skies. I would teach Misim how to play basketball and watch Ami's eyes grow wide at the sight of supermarkets as big as a whole shopping mall. I would be their guide, and together we would share this new adventure. And perhaps they would even begin to understand what had happened to me there. Perhaps I could finally explain the reason behind the change.

It had been a very different Ali Husnain who had made the trip to England a year and a half earlier. I started it full of confidence and ambition, and I returned with the most wonderful secret igniting my heart. But it was a secret that almost cost me my life. Now my confidence had vanished and the most noticeable thing about my heart was the scar slanting off the side of it. And as for that secret, it was no longer hidden. Everyone knew—from my friends to my teachers, from Baba-jan's business contacts to the militants who called me *kafir* and who claimed that the Qur'an gave them the right to kill me.

17

I tried to forget about them and think about what was coming next. I looked at the planes now overhead, flying higher and higher into the blue. I thought about how I'd soon be soaring toward a safe place, a new start.

I could hardly wait to see Ami and Zainab. My legs couldn't carry me fast enough as we walked to the terminal, and I started skipping along like Misim as we wove our way through taxis, rickshaws, and buses. I was a child again, excited beyond measure, my insides churning so much I thought they might make me float up into the sky.

The moment I saw them—standing just inside the far entrance— was the moment I finally gave in and started running. I was laughing and crying too, unable to hold in any longer the joy and relief of this reunion. In Ami's arms I felt everything fall away, all the fear and confusion. There in her embrace, the smell of her hair beneath her *hijab* filling my lungs, I was safe. I was in a crowd of thousands, but I was finally home.

I stepped back, my chest taking in deep gulps of air. Zainab held me for a bit too but soon busied herself with helping Misim as he returned the luggage trolley on which sat a single bag.

A single bag.

"Where is the rest of the luggage?" I asked. Even though I already knew the answer, it hit me like a gut punch.

"Nomi," said Ami, tears heavy in her eyes, her hands reaching out to hold mine. She was struggling to find the words, and Baba-jan had to step in and explain.

"They didn't get their visas yet. But they will follow you as soon as they can. It will not take long."

The news left me hollow. All the lightness and joy vanished. The smell that had comforted me was snatched from my senses. There would be no family adventures in England. I was being sent away not to rebuild a new life but to be erased from my old one. My worst fear was coming true.

I must have been in shock, for I don't remember much about the time we spent together at the airport before I finally said goodbye. I know we sat on cold metal chairs and ate in cold silence, but the taste of the food escaped me. All I could think about was the fact that I was too distracted by the reality that was slowly coming into focus: this could be the very last time I ever saw my family.

Of all the troubles I'd been through in the weeks leading up to that moment, this one was the worst. The realization of how final our goodbyes would be was like poison within me. And while Baba-jan talked about life at home and Misim ate up the food left on my plate, I knew Ami was thinking the same thought too. In her silence, in her sorrow, in the way she squeezed my hand tight beneath the table, I knew she understood.

Eventually it was time to go. Baba-jan handed me an envelope. "Look," he said, opening it, "visa, money, and tickets too. It's an open return, but you won't need to use it for a long time."

I glanced at them all. Everything seemed to be correct—the visa looked just like the one I received the first time I visited England, and the ticket was just as he said, an open return. But to me it felt like a one-way sentence. Why had he even bothered to buy a return ticket? I tried to suffocate my tears and will my feet to follow my family as they stood up and walked toward departures.

There were no crowds or long lines to slow my progress, no last-minute cancellation of flights to give me a reprieve. There were just two policemen on either side of the doors that led through to security, checking passports and tickets and hurrying people through.

Zainab handed me my case. "I put in some of your favorite things," she said. "Say hello to Aunt Gulshan for me." We embraced briefly before she stepped back. Misim held on for longer, but he pulled away too. Baba-jan offered a hand and an arm around my shoulders, while Ami held on the longest. It was an embrace in which I felt helpless and lost, like the smallest child I had ever been.

"It is time now," said Baba-jan, his arm guiding me toward the police and the doors between them. I picked up my case and walked. It felt light in my hands, too light for a journey like this. As I reached the guards, I turned and looked back. Zainab, Misim, Ami, and Baba-jan were standing together, a tight knot of four against the human traffic that flowed around them.

We stared at each other. Someone approached me and asked whether I was going in, but I waved them on ahead. I never took my eyes off my family, and their stares were just as strong. More people came up and I waved them on ahead of me as well, determined to steal as many seconds as I could from this moment. The noise of the airport grew louder—crowds, announcements, trolleys being pushed this way and that. It all threatened to drown me, but I fought it as best I could.

"What are you doing?" One of the policemen was at my side. He stepped in front of me, breaking the last thread of contact I had with my family. "You cannot wait there any longer. Go through."

Startled, I turned and walked through the doors. Ahead were more crowds and machines and police and noise, but I was desperate for one last look before I gave myself up to them. I turned back to see that the mirrored doors had closed behind me. Instead of my family, all I could see were the crowds of people hauling their bags onto conveyor belts and waiting to pass through scanners. In front of them I saw my own reflection. I looked small and tattered, just like my bag. My face was not my own, my eyes swollen with tears.

That's when I knew I was utterly alone.

How could anything be worth so much pain and loss?

The policeman returned to my side and ushered me into a line of people. I heard the doors behind me open again, but I knew there was no point in looking back through them.

I knew my family would be gone.

CHAPTER 1

KIDNAPPED

The first time I was kidnapped was so very different from the second. Both occasions filled me with terror, but it is the first that still revisits me in my nightmares. Perhaps it is because I was just four years old at the time. Perhaps it is because this was the exact point when I—still too young to properly tie my own shoes—learned that life can be a very dangerous affair. More likely it is because the kidnapper was my own father.

It happened on a day so hot I feared the sun would swallow the earth. The summer had conquered the dry earth, the empty sky, and everything in between. I remember feeling scared to venture outdoors.

"Nomi!" hissed Ami, "put your shoes on now." Usually, as I fumbled with the leather laces, Ami gave me gentle words of encouragement. Sometimes she even joined me in a little dance of celebration once I finally laced up each shoe. She was always like that with me—kind, patient, endlessly fun, somewhere between a mother and a big sister. Never once in those early years did I ever have cause to doubt the strength of her love for me.

But something was different about her on the day I was kidnapped. Her voice was strained and quiet, and she was not standing patiently by my side. Instead she was moving about inside the house, running from one room to another, calling for Zainab to get Misim—just a tiny baby in those days—and join us. Even at four years old, I was aware that something was wrong.

I recall my sister's high, thin cries for our mom to come and get her. I remember Ami's urgent replies and my own grunts of frustration as the shoes refused to cooperate. And there is another sound in my memory, a deep rumble, an angry shout like rocks tumbling down a mountainside. It was my father's voice—my real father, not my stepfather, Baba-jan. He was a terrible man.

I remember him starting to shout and seeing Ami reappear in front of me, urging me again to hurry. *"Jaldi, jaldi!"* She disappeared from my sight and I returned to my task, pushing and pulling but every time meeting with failure. The heat was too much and I wanted to lay down and sleep, but I knew I had to keep trying. Eventually I grabbed my shoes, and ran from the house to find her.

The shouting led me to the courtyard. As soon as I entered it, it felt as though the glare of the sun turned my eyes inside out. Blinking, I saw him, the dark shadow of a man that was my father, standing at the front of a crowd of people. With one hand he was pinning Ami by the throat, pushing her up against a wall. With his free hand he was hitting her, shouting with every blow he landed. The crowd cheered, and though there only could have been about fifteen of them, to my ears they were as loud as an army.

The heat robbed my mouth of moisture and my lungs of air, but from somewhere I managed a scream. That must have been what stopped my father's fist, and in the moment's pause, Ami twisted free, ran toward me, and swept me up in her arm as she passed. I remember that it felt like flying and that I liked it.

Only once we were beyond the gate at the back of our home was I placed on the ground again. Ahead of us were irrigated fields and a narrow elevated path that stretched out between them. "Run!" she screamed as she raced on ahead of me, Misim bundled in her arms, Zainab at her side. The path looked narrow to me and my legs were slowed by the heat of the soil and the fear of falling into the water on either side. I could hear my father's shouts behind me, a bear chasing his prey, his curses of Ami getting louder and louder. I tripped once, my hands stinging on a rock that had been well baked in the sun. I tripped again and saw blood well up on my palm. A third time and I lost my shoes. I turned back to get them and looked up to see men chasing. At the head of the pack was my father. I turned back to see that Ami had stopped and was pleading, "Leave him! Leave him!"

Then I was flying again. My legs left the ground and I found myself pressed against my father's side. He smelled odd. Unfamiliar. There was a ride in a strange car and a house I'd never been to before. A room with a door whose handle was too high for me to reach. I remember being hungry and thirsty and wondering why nobody came when I shouted. Eventually there was silence. I slept on one of the dark rugs that covered the floor and smelled like dust and dogs.

I don't know how many days I was kept in that room, but I know I wasn't well when I was finally rescued. It was Ami's brother who found me. My uncle was a policeman in Lahore, which meant he had both the contacts and the authority to disrupt my father's scheme. But even he was surprised by the state I was in. He says I was tearstained and nervous in the room, that my trousers were soaked and heavy and gave off a stench so foul he thought he might be sick.

After the kidnapping, Ami did something women in Pakistan simply do not do. She filed for divorce. A Pakistani woman remains where she has been placed, under the authority of her husband and his family. She is not supposed to question her husband's actions or resist his assaults. She is his property and can be treated however he wishes.

For those who try to escape an abusive marriage, the consequences can be severe. They can expect opposition and an increase in violence— even murder is not uncommon. And for the lucky few who manage to gain a divorce, the uncertainty and risk are far from over. In Pakistan, a single woman is about the most vulnerable person on earth, especially when she has brought it on herself.

Years later Ami told me that she did not take the decision to divorce my father lightly, yet she had been brought up to expect more from a husband than violence and verbal abuse. Like any Sayed woman, my mother stood out from the crowd, having been brought up wealthy. But she'd been shaped by more than money, for she'd received an education that had bred in her the expectation that people would treat her with respect even though she was female. Sadly, her breeding was a double-edged sword, and her family arranged for her to marry a man of similar social standing, another Shah. It didn't matter that she was in love with a different man; her father chose for her, and she knew better than to question him.

So while my father had the name, he didn't have the character, and it didn't take long for his hatred and disrespect to surface. For years my mother absorbed his punches and threats. But when it became clear that my father was prepared to use me, his firstborn son, in his games, Ami was compelled to act.

As soon as I was rescued by my uncle and Ami filed for divorce, she moved Zainab, Misim, and me to live with her in our grandmother's house on the edge of a small town hours away. I was happy there. The land stretched all the way to the horizon, and I played among the animals that wandered across the roads and fields in search of food. I learned how to drink milk straight from the cow and how to get to safety whenever I encountered a snake. I found that it was easy to get a herd of goats or sheep to go where I wanted them and learned that inviting a pack of dogs into the yard only ever ended in trouble.

I was the kind of child who could never sit still. On the rare occasions we went out to attend a family wedding or other important event, the battle of getting me dressed in a smart, clean *shalwar kameez* was enough to make Ami cry out with frustration. First she had to get me into the house, usually with a mix of bribes and threats. Next she had to get me to cooperate enough to wear the garments, and predictably I never liked formal clothes when I was young; they felt too much like chains across my back. I would wriggle and writhe as best I could to keep free of them. Ami always won, at which point she would stand back, arms crossed in victory. "Now," she'd say, "I want you to stay here on this bed and do not move while I get Misim ready." It was all the opportunity I needed. Within seconds I'd be back outside, jumping triumphantly in a puddle or throwing chickens high into the air.

Eventually Ami decided that life would be better for both of us if she let someone else try—and fail—to tame me. When I was just six years old, Shazi came to live with us. She was about five years older than me, and her job was to make sure I kept out of trouble. She was no match for me. I could slip away from her faster than I could Ami, and she was powerless to stop me from going outside whenever I wanted.

The world outside my grandmother's house exerted a strong pull on me and my curiosity grew stronger with each year that passed. Beyond the rusted metal gates at the front of the compound, I met so many different people—the shepherds, the men selling food, and the ones who fixed trucks, cars, and motorbikes out on the roadside. But it was the young man with the sodas who was my favorite. He was too poor to afford decent clothes, and it was his crippled leg that first caught my eye. It was thinner than the other, and when he staggered along, it hung limp beside the piece of wood he used as a crutch. But every day, he was there, sitting in the shade of the mandarin tree, with dusty unopened bottles of soda laid out neatly before him. At first I just watched him, observing how happy he seemed to be no matter what number of sodas he sold each day. Soon I joined him, sitting in the dirt beside him, neither of us talking much at all. His contentment was infectious, and it was enough just to be with him, watching all the typical dramas play out on the street in front of us. From time to time someone would come and buy a drink, and I would leap up and make sure the sale was conducted well. I suppose I wanted to protect him.

Whatever my motives, it was all too much for Ami.

"Why are you spending time with that man, Nomi?" she asked one day after I returned.

The question caught me off guard. I had never thought to ask it of myself. I just spent time with him because I liked spending time with him, that was all.

"Do you want to grow up to be like him?"

That was a question I had less trouble answering, and looking Ami right in the eye, I delivered my verdict: "Yes!" After all, he was happy. It seemed like a perfectly sensible ambition to me.

"No!" said Ami, delivering a swift but gentle blow to my head. "You will study and work hard and grow up to be a success. You are a Shah and a Sayed. You have potential in you, Nomi. You cannot waste it."

I didn't see myself as being worthy of any great ambition, but I understood a little about the potential within me, especially when it came to making trouble.

The electricity supply was especially poor in rural areas back then, and most days the power would be off from late in the evening until the wee hours. It suited me just fine, as it meant that when the day's heat had finally lessened I was able to play outside under cover of darkness—perfect conditions for my favorite game. I'd walk through the gates of neighbors' houses, creep silently to their front doors, and tape down their doorbells. Nothing would happen at that moment, but as soon as the power came back on later that night, the occupants would find themselves awakened by the never-ending scream of their doorbell. Sometimes I'd even lie awake and listen for the one-note symphony, smiling to myself in the darkness.

The heat of the day could be well in excess of 100 degrees, but when I was not at school, I rarely took Ami's advice to come inside or find some shade. My friends and I liked being up on the roof. From there we could see across the whole of the town. From there we could see the kites.

Kites mattered. Where American children challenge each other on the basketball court or in front of a gaming console, children throughout Pakistan and beyond duel with kites. We flew them for entertainment and pleasure, but so much besides: for glory, for honor, for the sweet taste of victory. When the wind was up and the rains absent, it seemed to me as though the whole sky was full of them. When the wind was getting up, I would beg Ami for one or two rupees, pleading with her to be allowed to go visit the man who lived on the main road that led out of town. Like every Shia household, he had what we called a *bhetak*—a formal room at the front or side of the house where non–family members could come and be shown hospitality without compromising the honor of any girls or women in the main house. Along with the very best furniture—heavy sofas and *charpai* beds for overnight guests—this man's *bhetak* was full of kites. He made them himself, and if you were lucky, he'd let you watch as he sat cross-legged on the floor, his hands a blur as he bent, glued, and twisted paper and cane together.

With a new kite tucked carefully under my arm and Misim and a friend or two following close behind, I'd head back home and take up position on the roof, ready to compete. We all knew how to fight with other kite flyers, and the technique is simple to understand, but almost impossible to master: when you spy an opponent, you must allow your kite to approach at just the right angle and speed, jerking and twisting at just the right time and in just the right way so that the string that stretches out between your hands and your own kite will strangle and slice through theirs. The winner is the last kite in the sky.

I often did okay as long as the other boys were flying kites like mine. If I was up against one that was tethered with the special sort of string that had been coated in glue and broken glass like they sold in Lahore for fifty rupees, victory was never a possibility.

I went to the roof to fly every day I could. And even if I had no kite and no money, I would still watch, hoping that somehow a freshly cut kite would land somewhere nearby. And even if that didn't happen, just gazing up at the way the air danced with brightly colored triangles was enough of a distraction to make an hour or two happily drift by.

It took a few years for the divorce to finally come through, and by the time Ami was summoned to court for the final time, I was old enough to accompany her and understand a little of what was going on. I had joined her on many of her visits to the lawyer's offices, and I liked the fact that she wanted me at her side. As her firstborn son I had certain responsibilities, and even though I was only just in double digits, I felt ready to face my father.

In the years we'd lived at my grandmother's, I had become Ami's confidant, listening as she told me more about what life was like before I was born. She told me that she had been forced to marry when she was eighteen years old and that it wasn't only my father who had beaten her but his brothers as well. These stories made me angry and I wanted to protect her, but somehow I knew revenge wasn't possible. It was just like it was with the kites; Ami—like all women in Pakistan— was a one-rupee kite in a sky full of men who could cut her down with their fifty-rupee strings. Though I was angry with my father for all he had done, I was just glad he was out of our lives.

That is why, when we arrived at court and I saw my father for the first time in five years, I merely nodded politely at him. I looked around the room at the dirty windows, the dark wooden tables set apart in front of the judge, the ceiling fans that stirred the air. I listened as the judge spoke and allowed my mind to drift to thoughts of what life was like for my father. Was he sad about what had happened? Did he miss his children? Did he wish things could be different?

I didn't have to wait long for my answer. The atmosphere in the room shifted, as if someone had cut the fans. All eyes were on my father as the judge addressed him.

"And I understand that you waive all rights to see your two sons and daughter in return for sole ownership of the house in Rawalpindi. Am I right?"

"That is correct, Your Honor."

I looked at my father. He was so much shorter than I remembered him. It struck me that his little mustache looked silly on him—far too small for someone so skinny—and that at his age, he looked more like a grandfather than a father. He wanted the house more than he wanted his children. Though I had entered the court wanting nothing more to do with him, this rejection still hurt.

The judge carried on speaking until the proceedings were over. Ami whispered to me that the terms were all agreed and the divorce was official when my father spoke up. "Your Honor, may I be allowed to take a photograph with my children?"

The judge looked perplexed but agreed, and seconds later I was pushed up out of my seat to stand at the front of the courtroom with my father sweating in the midday heat next to me.

"I'm your dad," he said as he prepared his hair for the photo. "I'm going to visit you every day." I knew he was saying it for show. At least, I hoped he was. He looked like he was trying to stand taller, but I was already almost his height. I knew it wouldn't be long before I outgrew him.

CHAPTER 2

GROWLING IN THE NIGHT

With a name like mine, so much of my childhood mischief went unpunished. My reputation preceded me. Life treated me and my family, an extended network sprawling across the region, with luxury. People looked up to us, even envied us. Only occasionally, that jealousy put us at risk.

Of all my cousins, Sharib was the one I liked the most—an expert in flying kites and playing on a building site, a master of getting into trouble and a genius at getting out of it.

Though he was older than me, he was a little shorter. He moved quickly, never sitting still, never resting. When he came over for the day and everyone else in the house was wilted by the heat, Sharib would be whirling like a sandstorm from one activity to the next. Most of the time his target was the young man of eighteen that his family employed to drive them around. I don't recall his name, though I can picture his patchy mustache and the permanently weary look upon his face. One of us would set off the car alarm and watch him run out from the *bhetak* in which he passed so many hours. While he was out, Sharib and I would enter the room and, in a matter of seconds, unleash the full extent of our chaos. The driver would return, survey the room with its upended table and cushions hurled around like bombs, and then sigh briefly before getting on with the task of clearing it all up as Sharib and I danced out of the room in celebration.

The best thing about spending time with Sharib wasn't the mischief we got into at my house. It was watching the crowds that flocked around his. Sharib's father, Uncle Haafiz—one of Ami's cousins—was a *zakir*, a religious teacher who was popular across the country. He had a jungle of thick black hair that fell to his shoulders and a stern face but kind voice. I was never quite sure whether I should fear or trust him. Uncle Haafiz and his family lived a couple of hours from me, and whenever I visited them I left feeling like a new person, a wiser one, with a wider view of the world.

It wasn't just that their home was big, with wide gates that opened onto a large courtyard. I loved the fact that above the main door of the house Uncle Haafiz had slung an *alam* or flag: a large rectangle of black with a white hand depicted beneath the words *Ya'Ali*, proclaiming that they were good Shia Muslims and devoted followers of Muhammad's first true disciple, Ali, my namesake. I would stare at it for hours, thinking about the words that Uncle had said to me once. "Do you know why it is black?"

"No, Uncle," I said.

"It should remind us that we are mourning the death of Ali."

Uncle Haafiz wasn't just any old *zakir*, he was famous and much loved. He had a way of retelling stories from Scripture that made the characters come alive. So many times I sat and listened as he told assembled crowds about important episodes that were the foundations of the faith. Sometimes as I listened I would look about me, taking in the sight of hundreds, sometimes thousands, of people all staring at my uncle with tears brightening their faces.

Best of all I loved to hear him tell the story about Muhammad's great-granddaughter Sakina and the time she asked her uncle Abbas to fetch water for her and the other children who were trapped in a camp by the enemy soldiers of the brutal leader Yazid. Abbas fought bravely to reach the river, but on the way back to camp he was attacked. Bloodshed followed, and soon Sakina was captured and eventually died. She wasn't much older than four years old. I could close my eyes and picture the scenes as if they were happening right in front of me. And nearly always I—like all the others—would end up sobbing.

For Muslims, there have been a number of prophets of God. Adam, Abraham, Moses, and Jesus are the first four, while Muhammad is the last. Muhammad's daughter, Fatimah, had two sons—Hasan ibn Ali and Husayn ibn Ali—and it is to these that all Sayeds can trace their lineage. Such a connection brings Sayeds honor and respect, and for those who are also well-known teachers like Uncle Haafiz, it brings *mureed*—disciples.

His followers would gather in his courtyard after they had been to the mosque and wait patiently for him to appear and sit with them. Some would ask for prayer, others would bring him gifts, and some were just happy to touch his leg or his knee in the hope that my uncle's mere touch would be enough to help.

My family had *mureed* too, though since the death of my grandfather a few years before my birth, their numbers had been falling. He had been a *zakir* too, and Ami had told me once that at the height of his fame he had as many as two or three thousand *mureed*. Sometimes as I looked out at the tiny knot of a dozen people in our own courtyard on a Friday afternoon, it was hard to imagine our family ever having so many and I wondered why our followers were so few in number compared to those of Uncle Haafiz.

"Ami, I don't understand," I said one day after returning home from school. "Uncle Haafiz has all those *mureed*. Why don't we get a big flag like his over our house?"

Ami was always patient with my questions. "Nomi, it's not just a matter of showing it with a flag; we have to show it with our lives. Besides, I don't want you to get into that life."

"What life?"

"Deciding not to study or work, living off the money the *mureed* give you."

"But these people respect their *zakir*. If we had more *mureed*, we would have more respect too. It is our identity."

Ami shrugged in a way that told me the conversation was over. "We should pray; that is our identity."

Her reasons for not wanting to parade our family's status went deeper than simple humility. As a divorced woman from a wealthy family living with a widow and a handful of children, Ami knew we were vulnerable. Anything that might draw too much attention to ourselves was an unnecessary risk.

We encountered many reminders of this reality throughout the time we lived with my grandmother. For a while someone from the town decided to keep ringing our doorbell at four in the morning. Whenever it happened, Qasim, one of our servants, would wake up and answer it, finding nothing but an empty doorway and the sound of feet and laughter disappearing into the night. At first I wondered whether it was retribution for my own pranks from years before, but after it had gone on for a few nights, Ami finally had enough and brought matters to a close. I woke up to the sound of the bell, but instead of the usual soft padding of Qasim's feet, I heard Ami crashing downstairs and hauling open the door. "What!" she shouted into the air. "You're too afraid to face a woman?"

I heard a muffled shout in response, a man's voice not far off. I heard Ami shout and then run out of the house. I guessed she was going to chase whoever had been harassing us, and I decided that as the eldest male I couldn't let her go alone. I jumped downstairs and followed her.

The air was still warm as I ran to catch up with her, and I was surprised to see a handful of buildings with the lights still on, each of them accompanied by the familiar growl of a diesel generator. Ami was fast and had a good head start on me, but my little legs were well used to short sprints. "Ami!" I called when I was nearly level with her, but she didn't stop. She was approaching a restaurant that was spewing light onto the street. The plastic tables out front were nearly all occupied, but Ami wasted no time marching up to one in particular. She stood in front of a man who remained seated, shouted something I couldn't hear, and bent down to remove her shoe before proceeding to beat him soundly with it. I'd stopped running at this point and was happy just to watch Ami humiliate him so, thrashing him repeatedly with her shoe. As we walked back to the house together, all I could say was, "Ami, you hit him with a *shoe*!" She just smiled like she always did and told me to hurry back to bed.

I knew it wasn't just drunken fools we needed to be wary of, for Ami kept a gun. She shared her bedroom with Zainab, Misim, and me, and if I was still awake when she went to bed, I'd watch through half-closed eyes as she reached up to the high shelf at the top of her cupboard, bring out the pistol, and place it under her pillow. I suppose it seemed just another part of life as I knew it, and I only ever questioned her about it once. "We have it because bad people are often scared by strength." So to me it was a logical decision, and having a gun was a guarantee that we would be kept safe.

But I never expected her to actually use it.

One afternoon, when Sharib and I were watching TV, we heard the sound of three gunshots upstairs. We exchanged horrified glances before both running toward the bedroom. Inside I saw Qasim lying on the floor, his arms covering his head, while Ami stood on the other side, a shocked expression on her face and the pistol lying on the floor in front of her.

"What happened, Ami?" I asked. "Are you okay?"

She couldn't talk at first, and it was Qasim who spoke up as he climbed up from the floor and rubbed his ears. "I asked, 'Madam, you have a gun, but do you know how to use it?' Your mother fired first into the ceiling but the recoil was too strong for her, and she fired two more shots straight ahead of her. I had to duck to avoid being shot."

Directly above Ami was a small hole in the ceiling, while ahead of her—directly above where Qasim had taken cover—were two more holes in the wall. I decided then to petition Ami not to sleep with the gun anymore. Clearly it was best left hidden away in case of emergency.

Though our family had known wealth and influence, we had also known more than our fair share of death. Ami had two brothers, but just after I was born, the elder one died, leaving no wife or children of his own. That left one brother, Uncle Shah, the same man who was a policeman in Lahore and who had rescued me from my father after he kidnapped me. He was a kind man, and throughout the time that Ami tried to divorce my father, he was a constant source of support and strength. His wife, however, was not happy about it. She was jealous and believed that Ami had brought shame upon the family by leaving her husband.

Things got even worse when my grandfather died suddenly, leaving the vast majority of his considerable wealth to my uncle. I was only eight at the time, unaware of the way that the love of money was causing hatred and evil to grow like a weed among people, and I had no idea that the fighting between my uncle and his wife increased. Even so, when he died of a heart attack shortly after my grandfather, nobody thought it was anything more than a cruel accident. At least, that is, until something truly strange happened to me.

I had escaped from Shazi for the hundredth time in order to play outside, so it was a day like any other. I was doing nothing unusual—just chasing some goats around the land beyond the house with a stick—when I slipped without reason and fell. The pain was immediate, a burning agony that sent fire down my leg and deep waves of nausea up through my stomach. Thankfully Shazi had already come out to try to find me, and she was able to pick me up and carry me back inside.

It wasn't the first time I'd experienced such pain. Even though I was young, I had already broken more bones than any of my friends. Twice I had broken my hand and once I had broken my leg, the same one now sending pain raging throughout my body.

"What were you doing, Nomi?" Ami asked as she gently ran her hands across my leg as I lay on the sofa inside. I couldn't offer any kind of reply, for by now the pain was so great I was sobbing. Even if I had been able to catch my breath, I wouldn't have been able to explain. Just like every other time I had broken a bone, the whole thing was a mystery to me. People accused me of being wild, but I knew that I had done nothing dangerous at all.

Eventually I must have calmed down enough to go to sleep, for the next thing I remember is waking up in the medical clinic, where a doctor with warm hands was setting my leg.

Ami asked me about the accident repeatedly over the coming days, and all I could say in reply was that I wasn't doing anything other than running along after the goats when I fell. "Was there a hole or a rock that you tripped over?"

"No, Ami," I said. "I just fell. I have no idea why."

If I'd simply gone on to recover from the accident, then perhaps Ami wouldn't have thought anything of it, but something was making her curious. A few nights after the accident, her suspicions were proved right as she heard me start to thrash around in my bed. I have no memory of what happened, but the story was often repeated to me in the years that followed. Apparently I began calling out in a voice that nobody in the house recognized as my own. It was a deep voice, more like a man's than an eight-year-old boy's. I was angry to the point of scaring people, almost growling, raging against something—just what, no one knew.

"It is a *jinn*," said Qasim eventually. "We should talk to it."

Ami did as he suggested, trying to talk to the spirit and find out what it wanted, yet she got little response.

The next day I had no recollection of the episode, though my leg hurt and I was tired. The family gathered and discussed what was to be done. All agreed that if it really was a *jinn*, some kind of sacrifice needed to be made to appease it. So they bought a black goat, slaughtered it, and threw it into the graveyard, hoping that whatever spirit was troubling me would be satisfied with the meal.

That night I started to growl and shout again. The goat hadn't helped at all, and as the house filled with the unnatural sounds coming from my little body, Ami started to worry. She called the *mullahs* from the mosque and asked their advice. "Leave him with us," they said. "We will take the boy and beat him for three days. That will get rid of the *jinn*."

Ami had a better idea.

When the next night came and I started shouting again, she leaned in close to me, placing her hand on my head and speaking softly. "Nomi, it is me, Ami. What do you see?"

"I see Uncle," I said in my own voice. "He is in the bathroom, about to take his medicine, but someone has changed it."

"Who?"

"Aunty. She is the one who has changed his pills."

At that, I started thrashing around, my arms and both legs—even the broken one—whirling and pushing back everyone who was near me. It took Ami, Qasim, my grandmother, and a couple of other neighbors who had visited to hold me down. They say that I fought with the strength of a grown man.

It was only on the fourth day that something happened I will never forget. I was dozing in the afternoon, feeling a little weak and a lot sorry for myself, wondering how long it would be before I would be able to return to my games outside.

"Nomi," said a voice I didn't recognize. "How are you?"

I looked up to see a lady wearing sunglasses and brightly colored clothes. "This is Aunt Gulshan," said Ami, standing to one side. Up until this point, I didn't know I had an aunt Gulshan. But the woman looked nice enough. "I am well, I think," I said.

"I would like to pray for you. Would you let me?"

I had been around lots of people who asked for prayer—mainly the *mureed* outside Sharib's house. They would ask for a prayer and Uncle Haafiz would either touch them briefly before moving on or tell them that he would remember them the next time he was at prayers. I had never been asked whether I would allow someone to pray for me before. But something told me that there was only one answer I could possibly give. "Yes," I whispered.

Aunt Gulshan knelt down beside me. She kept her sunglasses on and I remember both wishing that she would take them off and being relieved that she did not. She placed her hand on my head and I flinched immediately. It was as if her touch somehow released a great heat in my skin. It was hot—hot with strength, but not with pain. "Do not worry," she said. "It is okay." Her voice was soft and low.

She started to pray, but again things were different. I had only ever heard people pray in Arabic before. That was our formal religious language, the tongue spoken by Muhammad himself, but Aunt Gulshan was praying in Urdu, the common language we used every day as we talked to each other and went about our business. Still, I felt calm and somehow relaxed by the gentle way the words fell from her mouth. She told the *jinn* to leave and asked God to speed the healing of my leg. The heat grew a little more intense and then died away. As it did, I felt the need to inhale deeply. Somehow the air felt better than it had for days, and every breath brought with it a deep, deep sense of calm.

That night I slept soundly. The *jinn* never returned. And after Ami confronted her sister-in-law with the news of what I told her I had seen, she never saw her again. She never did get the money she was after.

CHAPTER 3

NEW HORIZONS, NEW DANGERS

It was one of those mornings you wake, dreams fading as you stretch your stiff limbs, and walk downstairs into a world that has changed completely overnight.

Two months earlier Ami, Misim, Zainab, and I had moved away from my grandmother's house in the quiet village to a new house in the bustling city of Lahore. It signaled the start of a new phase in my life, in which I felt like I was living inside some kind of fantasy world.

First, there was the new home. It was a palace, easily the biggest place in the neighborhood. It was also brand new, and some of the building work was still going on when we first arrived. We had to swap rooms from time to time to allow the small army of builders, plumbers, and painters to be able to finish their work. Ami had decided on a staggering total of fourteen rooms. For the first few days I would frequently get lost and have to carefully retrace my steps in order to reach my intended destination.

It did not occur to my twelve-year-old mind to question why Ami would want to build so big a home. I had no idea that our move from my grandmother's house was influenced by something other than a desire to have a little more space for us three children. All I knew was that once I got to know the place, I quickly fell in love with it. The way the courtyard was bathed in colored lights at night entranced me, and

I would stare for what felt like hours on end at the bright greens and deep reds as they washed over the broad-leaved plants and snakelike vines that had been carefully imported from miles away. There were water fountains whose gentle sounds washed through the windows on one side of the house, the biggest *bhetak* I'd ever seen; a guest room with a seating area so large it had eighteen ceiling fans hovering above it. The house was surrounded by a ten-foot-high wall with large metal gates at the front leading onto a wide courtyard, as well as a smaller set of gates at the back that opened onto a patch of wasteland. I liked the idea of being able to leave undetected and wander among the animals that grazed lazily among the weeds and shrubs. The cows, goats, and chickens belonged to our neighbors, but I liked to pretend they were all mine.

But what confused me as I sleepily crossed the tiled floor and descended the main staircase that morning was not the way the house looked, but the way it sounded. Instead of the noise of builders working in some distant room, I heard the unfamiliar sound of a crowd of women talking and laughing. I sat down a few steps up from the bottom and waited, hoping to be able to work out what was going on.

"What are you doing there?" said Zainab as she rushed down from behind me.

"I'm listening. There's something going on."

Zainab laughed. "Of course there is something going on. Ami's getting married today."

Her answer didn't make sense at first, but slowly its meaning came into focus.

"Who is she marrying?"

Zainab didn't laugh this time. Instead she looked carefully at me. "Muzafa Shah," she said, saying the two words slowly as if she were talking to little Misim.

This was not a stranger's name. I knew the man well. Muzafa Shah was the tall lawyer with the Western suits and the thick black hair who had helped Ami get her divorce. I had visited his office many times with Ami, and he had always been helpful and kind. Yet I felt no great joy at the news. I was too surprised for that.

I got up from the step and followed Zainab as she walked the length of the hall that led to the kitchen. There must have been thirty women at work there, and the noise was a little overwhelming. I looked for Ami but couldn't find her anywhere. But back in the large room with the eighteen ceiling fans, I found a line of tables that ran the length of the wall. I stared for a couple of minutes at the food laid out on them. There were large plates full of sweets like *gulab jamun*, little globes of milky sweetness; *barfi*, cubes rich with mango, coconut, and pistachio; and *kulfi*, or ice creams. There were samosas and *biriani*, and when I was sure the room was empty, I grabbed a handful and loaded my mouth, just before feeling a hand on my shoulder.

It was Ami. She was wearing a red *shalwar kameez* and *dupatta*, a long headscarf that caught the light as she walked. I was stunned at how beautiful she looked. Her happiness adorned her. "Nomi," she said, smiling at me. "You remember Mr. Shah, don't you?" A familiar figure appeared at her side. He was wearing white, like any groom would, and as he stood in front of me, I noticed how perfect his clothes were. Silver thread traced intricate patterns all over his outfit and he stood with all the confidence of a victorious military commander.

"Ali," he said, extending his hand. "I would like you to call me Baba-jan."

I nodded, swallowed my mouthful of cake, and shook his hand in return. "Yes, of course."

With a final kiss on the head, Ami sent me back upstairs to get dressed in the clothes that Qasim would soon lay out for me.

The rest of the day passed in a hazy, colorful blur. I enjoyed the sweets and the *naan* and the way that throughout the whole day whenever I approached Ami I inhaled sweetly perfumed air thanks to the garland of lavender and orange blossom she wore around her neck. But it was strange too. *Ami is now married.* I repeated the words to myself over and over. Perhaps eventually they would make sense.

The day after the wedding we watched as our luggage was loaded onto a truck and then climbed into a car and drove for hours, heading north for the mountains that lay beyond Islamabad. We stayed in the biggest hotel I had ever seen, a building so large it dwarfed any school, hospital, or government office I had seen before, even in a city as large as Lahore. It was a beautiful place to be, and we spent our days taking cable cars high up into the mountains and trekking our way back down, riding horses, and walking around the hotel grounds.

"Nomi," said Ami one afternoon as we were out walking. She and I had drifted back from the others and were alone for the first time since before the wedding. "Are you sad?"

I shrugged and told her I wasn't sure.

"Do you remember the story that I told you about how your father and I were married?"

"Yes. Your father arranged it all."

"That is right. And do you remember that I was not happy about marrying your father?"

"Yes."

"Do you remember why I didn't want to marry him?"

I remembered the sight of him with his fingers clenched tight around her throat, pushing her up against the wall. I remembered the sound of his fist as it hit her cheek. I remembered being alone and afraid and hungry. I stared back at Ami.

"I did not want to marry your father because I wanted to marry another man. His name was Muzafa Shah." She paused to allow the news to sink in a little.

"So," I began, thinking it through. "Baba-jan is the one you should have married all along?"

She smiled and held me to her, radiating orange blossom and lavender. "That's right, Nomi."

Gradually I got used to the idea of sharing Ami and the rest of my family with her new husband. It wasn't bad after all—Ami was happy, and when she was happy, so were we. When we returned home after the holiday in the mountains, I finally understood why Ami had built the house the way she did. It was perfectly symmetrical, with seven rooms on each side of the house. Though we lived in the house as if it was one home, I could see that it would be possible to split the house down the middle and make two smaller but perfectly good separate houses. When Zainab, Misim, and I grew up, Zainab would marry and move to her husband's home, while Misim and I would each bring our own wife to live with us in our respective side of the house.

Baba-jan, as I had to train myself to call him, brought more than respectability, wealth, and security with him. He was also a Shia and bore the name Ali and had *mureed* of his own. But where Ami's desire for religious humility had led her to be a little shy about the disciples who came to her mother's house, Baba-jan threw his arms open as wide as the front gates, welcoming all after Friday prayers.

The truth is that until Baba-jan became my stepfather, my knowledge of what it meant to be a Muslim was limited. I knew that Shia Muslims were the minority in our city and that most of my friends were Sunni, but it would take years before I truly began to understand the difference—as well as the violence—that separates the two.

The tension between the minority Shia and majority Sunni goes all the way back to the earliest days of Islam. In the years after Muhammad died, there were disagreements about who should lead the Muslim community. Some followed his son-in-law, Ali, while others looked to a man named Abu Bakr, marking the first division between Shia and Sunni. By the time Ali's own son Husayn assumed the role of leader, his opponent was a warrior named Yazid. At the Battle of Karbala, Yazid's forces killed Husayn and all his supporters, including his infant son. Centuries have passed since then, but the blood shed that day still stains our history.

I was seven when I first became aware of any of this. One day while I was out with my friends I heard the *adhan* ring out across the rooftops, and I thought nothing of following my peers into their Sunni mosque to pray. Ami was upset with me when I returned home and told her about the strange mosque where people said prayers in different ways, but it would be years before I understood how dangerous it can be for a Shia to do such a thing.

Baba-jan taught me much about what it meant to be Shia. He taught me that *mureed* were to be treated with respect but were a reminder of the responsibilities that any descendant of Ali must shoulder. "We must provide for their spiritual needs," he told me once as I stood next to him looking out the window above the front yard. "They are like wild goats that graze on our land. We don't own them, but we have a duty to look after them."

I understood what Baba-jan meant a little better when he told me that we were to have our first *majlis*—a whole-day event where all the *mureed* and hundreds of others would come and listen to different *zakirs* preach. I had been to one of them before, accompanying Sharib when his father was speaking at one in Lahore. It was a magical time, and though the crowd was large and loud and I could barely see the front stage when we first entered the room at the back, I trusted Sharib and followed him as he strode all the way to the very front. There, among the *mullahs* and all the other important guests, we saw Uncle Haafiz sitting on the stage. He nodded to us and invited us to sit close to him, not quite on the stage, but off to the side.

Some deep memories were carved into my mind that day. I watched the faces of the crowd—which must have been one or two thousand people in number—and saw each of them reflect the different moods that the *zakir* drew out of them. Some turned the room dark with shame as they issued stern reminders about purity. Others brought light and hope as they painted pictures of paradise and the future awaiting those found worthy. But my uncle was better than all of them. He didn't paint with just a single color; he used the whole spectrum. Like many, he sang as he preached, his voice rising and falling in the most powerful melodies, tracing great arcs in the sky like a hawk circling high overhead. He wove stories so powerfully that the whole room was enthralled. He took people back into history, placing them in the middle of events described in the Qur'an, making the characters come alive and getting to the very heart of what it means to be a Shia. He told stories about the prophet, about Ali, and about his grandson. He talked about Yazid's brutal massacre of innocents at Karbala, the siege of Mecca, and the murder and rape of ten thousand men and women at Medina—all key events that every Shia knows well. "What if it was your daughter?" he would ask. "What if it was you?" By the end, the air was thick with the sound of men sobbing.

And so, when Baba-jan told me that we too would be holding our own *majlis*, I was excited. When the day came, the gathering wasn't as large as it had been that day I visited Lahore, but the police did have to close off the street outside our house, and the crowd that spilled out into the courtyard must have been at least two or three hundred strong.

At the end of the *majlis*, just as the people started to leave and I noticed that the sound of the crickets could be heard again, I saw a man waiting off to the side a few feet in front of me. Our eyes met and he approached. He was in his twenties and looked as though he might have traveled far, but I could not be sure. He didn't look so poor as to be wearing rags, but neither did he look well off enough to have proper shoes.

"Husnain-ji," he said, using the most respectful form of address and bowing his head low. "I would like to ask you to pray for me."

Nobody had ever asked me to pray for them before, but I had seen enough people approach Uncle Haafiz and even Sharib to know what to say.

"Very well. What for?"

"I have no son. I would like for you to pray that I would have a son."

"Very well. I will pray," I replied, before remembering something

Sharib had said once. "I shall pray and Allah shall hear the prayer and you shall have a son."

The man muttered his thanks and left, and I went inside, forgetting to pray either then or at any other time. Did that make me a bad Muslim? Perhaps, but I was also just a child. I was not devout at that age, but I did know that I had been born into a privileged position within the faith. I knew I had a bright future ahead of me, perhaps even as a *zakir* myself one day.

Baba-jan enrolled me in a new school soon after he moved in. It was expensive and run by Catholics. Though not as infamous as India's caste system, Pakistan's society is also firmly structured, with everyone being fully aware of who is above and who is below them. And Catholics were way down the list. The only thing I knew about these quiet Christians was that they were meant to be good at music and ran good schools. Yet they were still *umti*, members of a lower caste than I was. They were not to be feared any more than they were to be abused or mistreated, but they were *umti* all the same.

I entered my teenage years with the knowledge that life was starting to get better. The Catholic school was going to provide me with a good education, Baba-jan was helping our family to regain some of its social standing, and the days when we were plagued by drunken fools knocking on our door at four in the morning were now just a distant memory. We even started to accompany Baba-jan to the country club, behind whose gates I found a whole new world of neatly trimmed lawns, gentlemen's sports, and polite company.

Yet something else also gave me reason to feel optimistic, even excited about the future, and it started one Friday after prayers when I looked out at the crowd in the courtyard and recognized a man standing nearby. It was the man who had approached me after the *majlis* and asked for prayer for a son. I felt a brief sting of guilt for not praying, but as soon as my eyes met his, he came over, a smile as wide as a kite spread across his face.

"*Husnain-ji*," he said, bowing briefly. "My wife has given me a son!"

I smiled back, relieved—and utterly surprised.

"I would like to give you a gift to show my thanks. What do you need?"

Without really thinking about it, I replied, "Well . . . I need dogs."

One month later he returned, one hand cradling a healthy son and the other—more excitingly for me—holding a pack of four of the most beautiful dogs I'd ever seen. They could only have been a few months old, and their wiry golden coats were as soft as silk. This was the beginning of what I liked to think of as my own personal zoo, and within a year or two I had added a pigeon, some chickens, and even a cow to my collection, keeping them all in the sprawling, enclosed back yard.

Where Baba-jan taught me about the duties and responsibilities of my caste, Ami was more concerned with my religious instruction. Like every good Muslim, I needed to learn how to read the Qur'an, yet unlike those who were poor and had to visit the *madrassa* after school for their lessons, we were able to afford to pay a *mullah* to come and visit all three of us children at home.

It suited me fine. School was full of talk about what went on in the *madrassa*, with rumors suggesting that some of the *mullahs* were violent and others were gay. Either way, I didn't much like the idea of being under their care for any amount of time, and I understood precisely what Ami meant when, on the afternoon before our first lesson, she said to me, "If he touches your sister or you, then let me know straightaway, yes?"

I agreed and was more than happy to act as an unofficial spy. I didn't fear the *mullah*, not when I was in my own house, and not when I made sure the door was always left open as Ami had suggested.

The *mullah* was an older man, his thick beard well flecked with streaks of white. His black robes were stained and smelled bad, and he did try to hit Zainab once during that first lesson when she failed to read a word correctly, but my shout of Ami's name and her stern words with him were enough to make sure that it never happened again.

The real problem with his lessons was that they were dull. Like every other Qur'an I'd seen, the copy he brought with him was written in Arabic. Being an educated Pakistani boy, I was already learning several languages—Punjabi among friends and street traders, Urdu at home, and English at school—but Arabic was by far the hardest. Our lessons consisted of nothing more than sitting in front of the book, which the *mullah* placed on a low table, and reading it out aloud. A few words were translated on the page, but the vast majority were not. So I had no real idea what I was saying. This bothered me, and I was continually asking the *mullah* what certain phrases meant.

"It is not for children," was his standard response. I wanted to go slow, to read through the passages at a pace that would allow me to try to tease out the meaning, but for my teacher this was not an option. *"Jaldi, jaldi!"* he would say, hurrying me along. As far as he was concerned, I was a failure at reading the Qur'an. "You read too slow," he grumbled, more than once. "Nobody will want to listen to you read if you carry on like that." But I had no interest in putting in a good performance or entertaining people. I was developing my appetite for the Qur'an and wanted to understand the truth behind it all, not learn the tricks of impressing people with my accomplished reading voice. After all, I had sat in enough meetings where Uncle Haafiz was preaching to know that it took more than entertainment to ignite something in the hearts of the listeners.

School was a strange place for me. I was academically average and not at all inclined to work hard at subjects that I found difficult. Why would I? My name alone would get me followers and a position of power within my local community, and my family's financial backing would allow me to become a businessman in my own right. By the time I became a teenager, I was growing accustomed to having *mureed* approach me on the street and ask for prayer, and every morning when I came downstairs Qasim would be waiting by the door, ready to pass me my bag as I left. My life outside school had all the potential and excitement, and it was obvious to me that there was little I could learn in a classroom that would prepare me for life after it. As soon as I gained some basic qualifications, I would be out in the world, setting myself up in some business or other.

Yet there were parts of school life I did enjoy, the times between lessons when I could spend time with my friends. We were a mixed bunch; only two of us were Shia, with the rest Sunni. That didn't make any difference, though. We were a select few, the sons of business leaders and local politicians, young men who were privileged by birth and who knew even at our young age that we would have an important role to play in society.

Like any group of adolescents, we were clear about who belonged with us and who did not. We reserved our worst words for anyone who was not a Muslim. To us they were a *kafir*—an unbeliever, an infidel. If we happened to pass by a TV set that was showing an American program, it would be only a matter of seconds before one of us called out, *"Kafir!"* and the rest of us would start nodding and murmuring our agreement. "They don't fear God," someone would inevitably add. "They are blind to the truth."

Calling someone a *kafir* was a risky thing. I hurled the term out at Sharib once when we still lived at my grandmother's house, and the force with which Ami beat me left me in no doubt that it was a mistake. Still, it was a useful lesson to learn in other ways, for when I was once thrown out of class for fighting with another boy and punished with several hits of a stick on the hand by one of the teachers, I had a ready-made excuse that I could tell Ami to dissipate her anger. Even before she got to the stage of shouting at me once she noticed the thick welts across my palm, I knew what my defense would be. "He called me a *kafir*" was enough to quell her rage in an instant.

Non-Muslims weren't the only people we defined ourselves against. We all were scared of the Wahhabi. These are the ultra-conservative Muslims, extremists who follow a set of teachings that have wandered far from traditional Sunni roots. Over the years Wahhabism has given birth to the Taliban, Al Qaeda, and more. They hate Westerners, whom they kill in gruesome terrorist attacks. And they hate Shia Muslims too.

The Wahhabi were highly visible around Lahore, dressed in conservative clothing and black or green turbans. I always tried my best to avoid them. From time to time I would see them at the house, there to conduct some business or other with Baba-jan. I always took care to drop my eyes, reach out to shake the hand they offered, and reply to their greetings with a polite *"Wa alaykum al-salaam."*

"They are not so bad," Baba-jan often said after they left. "We have nothing to fear from them."

Ami did not agree, and when the two of us were alone, she'd whisper warnings about the Wahhabi who visited us. "You must stay away from them," she would tell me. "They are not safe and things are getting worse for us Shia."

These warning conversations happened most often during the period known to all Muslims—other than Wahhabi—as Muharram. This annual event remembers the great Battle of Karbala in which Muhammad's grandson Husayn ibn Ali and most of his family and supporters were brutally slain by Yazid's forces after Husayn refused to pledge allegiance to Yazid.

So for all Shia, Muharram is a time of sorrow, a period when we gather for *majlis* to help us remember the sacrifice, courage, and honor of our ancestors. It is the time when we march in crowds as big as oceans and when some young men even whip themselves with chains until the blood covers not just their backs but the streets as well. We do it to remember the pain and bloodshed that have gone before us.

It might seem strange to admit it, but I always enjoyed Muharram. Though my Sunni friends would observe parts of the rituals too, we all knew the Shia would take the lead. I was often allowed to carry a flag in the great procession called a *jaloos*, or take a seat of honor on the stage at a *majlis* and listen to Uncle Haafiz as his voice brought great sobs from the crowds. I liked it too because it was one of the times when I was aware of just how much it mattered to be a good Muslim. The older I became, the more I understood why it was important to celebrate a man's honor and dignity as he sacrificed his life in the face of overwhelming terror. This kind of courage appealed to me. Celebrating this history gave me a sense of identity within a story greater than myself, something I hadn't realized I so deeply craved.

I was twelve years old the first time I was invited to carry one of the tall flags in a *jaloos*. Ami was not in favor of my taking such a visible part in things, but I sided with Baba-jan and thought it was a great idea. I had to concentrate hard to keep the wooden pole upright, and I used all the puny strength I could summon to hold it steady. "That is good," said Baba-jan as he stood beside me. Standing slightly behind a line of mullahs, I followed them as we all took our first steps on the march. The noise was incredible, and I was aware that behind me was a horde of people at least one thousand strong, and picturing them made me work even harder to lift the flag high. Gradually I found myself relaxing into the task, and by the time we neared the mosque and the end of the procession, I took a little pleasure in staring up at the way the black flag with the white hand caught in the gentle wind. It didn't matter that my arms were tired or that I'd become separated from Baba-jan or that the heat was starting to make my head spin. What mattered was that I carried out my task well, holding the flag straight and tall.

My focus broke the moment I heard the first person shout. I couldn't hear what they said, but the tone of their voice, and the effect it had on the crowd, told me that something was wrong. I looked back to see people running, scattering out from the procession in all directions. Close by I saw a young man climb onto a wall and shout, "There is a bomb!"

I did not stop to think or weigh the situation. I did not look for Baba-jan to seek reassurance or guidance. I simply dropped the flag and ran. Yes, I was a Muslim, a proud Shia. But I had no desire to die at the hands of a Wahhabi bomber.

I had seen enough news reports where bloodied corpses were scattered along the roadside amid rubble and broken glass to know this threat was real. It was common enough for big Shia religious festivals to come under attack, especially at a time like Muharram when memories of old feuds were revived. I ran stumbling, bracing myself for the explosion at any moment, but none came.

I was a mile from home but made it back through the narrow turns and twists that mapped out the neighborhood in a handful of minutes. Ami must have heard the shouts and sirens, for she was waiting for me, and I held tight for as long as I could. Together we looked down the road for Baba-jan. He was back soon after.

"What happened?" Ami asked.

"They found the bomb," said Baba-jan. He looked more weary than frightened, more irritated than enraged, as if this was more of an inconvenience than a brush with death. "It was hidden in a bush near the mosque. Are you okay, Nomi?"

I nodded. But inside, I was shaken. One moment I was marching proudly, waving high my flag in honor of a man who had died for what he believed in. A man who was my namesake. But the very next moment, I was running scared—unwilling to do the same.

CHAPTER 4

MURDER IN THE STREET

"Why would you want to drive a Honda when there is a Range Rover parked right next to it?"

Baba-jan's driver looked back at me, his hand frozen in front of the keys hanging from wooden pegs beside the door.

"You would look much better behind the wheel of the Range Rover, don't you think?"

I knew I had him already, but I carried on just to make sure. "Besides, Friday prayers will be ending soon and everyone will see you as we pass the mosque. You would like that, no?"

Persuading Baba-jan's driver to go against his better judgement and give in to my wishes was one of my favorite pastimes. But getting driven in the car of my choice was only the beginning. From the minute he pulled out of the gate, I would make it my mission to harass the poor man into letting me drive. He would try all the usual lines to dissuade me—reminding me that Baba-jan would not be happy, that it was illegal for me to drive at so young an age, and that my lack of height forced me to view the road through the narrow gap between the steering wheel and the top of the dashboard. Yet it was only a matter of time before he pulled over and let me drive the last block for myself.

Driving became something of a passion for me, even more so when Sharib turned up one day on his own motorbike. It had a set of chrome mudguards and a double seat that was big enough to transport four, and the fact that Sharib was too young to legally drive such a machine didn't seem to bother him, or anyone else for that matter.

Sharib's new bike signified the start of one of the best periods of my childhood. We were able to spend hours speeding around the dusty Pakistani countryside at will, wasting whole days drinking mango milk shakes and beating each other's high scores on Tekken at Uncle Faizal's video arcade. We might blow a hundred rupees on food for ourselves and any friends who were around, and we became so accustomed to fitting three or four of us onto Sharib's bike and driving around the city that we lost all fear of falling off.

During that year's Muharram, Sharib took us to the other side of the city to listen to his father preach. All the usual emotions flowed through me—a little pride, a lot of awe—but for the first time in a mosque I found myself thinking back to the bomb that had failed to go off during the procession the previous year. For the first time I started to feel unsafe.

Sharib and I and two of our friends left the *majlis* soon after it finished. The four of us arranged ourselves on the bike—Sharib in front, followed by the other two and me on the back—just as we had dozens of times before, letting our bodies relax and follow Sharib's lead as he rode. It was late and dark, and apart from the odd dog or worker sleeping in the street, Sharib's headlight picked out few signs of life.

We were midway between the mosque and my home when we were suddenly illuminated by headlights. I turned to see a car right up close behind us, its bright lights blinding me temporarily. I felt Sharib pick up speed for a moment before slowing down again. By the time I could open my eyes and see again, the light from behind us was flashing blue.

"You should not be out this late," said the officer as he stepped from the car and approached us at the side of the road. "There are Wahhabi about. It could be dangerous for you boys."

Sharib mumbled something about going home, but the policeman was not done.

"What are your names?"

We told him.

"How old are you?"

We told him, though not the truth this time.

"What do your fathers do?"

"My father's a lawyer," I said.

"And mine is a *zakir*," said Sharib.

"A surgeon."

"A politician."

The policeman looked hard at us. "They can come and get you from the police station," he said before pausing and staring at us some more. By this time we were all a good deal more relaxed and knew what he was thinking: *If any of these boys is telling the truth and either a* zakir, *lawyer, surgeon, or politician has to come to the police station to collect his son, it isn't the boys who will end up in trouble, but me.* He paused. "You had better phone them," he said before pausing again, clearly playing out this second scenario before concluding it was equally unwise. Eventually he thought better of that idea too and waved us on before returning to his car.

I became increasingly confident in myself. Like any teenager from my background living in a neighborhood like mine, I was able to visit most shops and get whatever I wanted without having to hand over any cash. It was enough simply to tell them that I would send my servant along later to settle the bill, and Qasim would always dutifully oblige.

Other boys, whether older or younger than my friends and me, would vacate the volleyball net or the patch of land on which we played cricket as soon as we turned up. I never had to fight, and I never wanted to. I was simply treated with respect. It never occurred to me that this was anything other than normal.

Though I was privileged, I wasn't exempt from certain chores that

Ami gave me. She would frequently come and find me lying around my room in the early evening and send me out to go buy chicken and roti cooked in the tandoor, fish that was fried in giant pans, or thick, rich goat *murgh* that bubbled away in smaller dishes down low on the street. While I loved to stand and watch the men as they spun the pans with one hand and agitated the food with the other, and would close my eyes and let both the sounds and the smells overtake me for minutes at a time, I loved video games more. So I would pause briefly in front of the street chefs and give them my order, with the additional instruction that they were not to make the food for another couple of hours, then head straight for Uncle Faizal's.

Uncle Faizal's was the center of our universe. As many as a hundred boys and young men could be crowded in around the four arcade machines that stood in the shop. Sitting on his high stool in the doorway, Uncle Faizal himself was part of the appeal. Though none of us ever saw him play on the machines, it was clear that at some point in his life he had been a committed gamer. He knew all the cheats and all the tricks, but treated novice and expert with equal politeness and respect. He had always been kind to me, right from my first visits when I could barely see the screens. But I had no special privileges over anyone else. He made sure everyone got their turn, even if it meant a long wait. In Uncle Faizal's, it suited me fine. His was a place of refuge, a room in which time stood still and nothing else in life mattered.

By the time I was old enough to see the screen and reach the controls comfortably, I could make the three tokens that a single rupee bought me last well over an hour. More than once, after I had been forced to wait in line for what seemed like forever and finally got the controls, I felt the familiar tug of Ami's hand on my shoulder just as I was about to defeat yet another kid playing next to me. She rarely said anything but looked at me with the kind of expression that drew from my lips a swift apology.

School continued to be a challenge. My friends and I were a wild bunch, and though we were happy enough to be there with each other, we would do anything we could to prevent the teachers from making us study. So we talked. A lot. Depending on the teacher, we would overwhelm them with inane questions, flattery, inflammatory statements, or just simple chatter among ourselves. To the less educated teachers we were "a class of animals" or "headed for trouble," while to others we were "rambunctious" and "far too full of ourselves."

Still, the school played along. They knew we all came from influential families, and they had no desire to lose our tuition. So when necessary, they bent the rules a little for us. I counted on this, especially when it came to the end-of-year exams.

A few days after one particular math exam for which I had done precisely zero study, Qasim announced that my teacher was at the door and wanted to talk with me and Ami.

"How do you think you got on?" the teacher asked as he, Ami, and I sat in the lounge.

"Me?" I shrugged before flashing a smile. "It was the best exam ever!"

The teacher stared at me. "You failed," he said.

Instantly deflated, I had nothing to say. All I could think was this meant I would have to repeat the year.

"But," said Ami firmly, "he has to pass."

The teacher looked uncomfortable as he considered the options. "Very well," he said. "I will leave the paper for you to complete at home then."

With the paper in my possession, the same one I had failed at school, I took my time and made sure I consulted with my cleverest friends before handing in the completed test. Nobody was surprised when I found out that I had passed, but the relief was tangible within me.

Even from a young age I was sure that I would do well in business. More than once throughout my childhood I had set up a stall outside my house and spent hours selling whatever item I was convinced would make me rich that day. The world was mine for the taking, or so

I thought. "Today it is kites," I would tell my customers, "but tomorrow it will be BMWs!"

In so many ways, life in Pakistan was small. I traveled out of Lahore a handful of times each year and had even been up north to Murree, but in truth my world began and ended with my neighborhood. It was there among the streets that Sharib and I rode around, among the people who spilled out of the mosques, among the street traders and businessmen alike, that I believed I would live and work. Sure, I imagined I would travel from time to time, but I never imagined I would stray far from the big house that Ami built. As the eldest son, I knew my future was to be played out there and nowhere else.

There was one exception to all this. I was fascinated by England. Everything from our education and legal systems to much of our architecture bears the mark of the British. As a result, English was the one subject in which I would pay attention at school, and England was the only other country I ever considered visiting.

My fascination with the country was made even deeper by my fascination with Aunt Gulshan. After she prayed for me and helped rid me of the *jinn*, she disappeared. Ami told me that she had returned to her home in England but would visit again. She was right, and every year she came back to Pakistan and stayed with us for a week or two. Between her strange ways of praying and her knowledge of life thousands of miles away, she was just about the most mysterious and interesting person I had ever met.

Like many Pakistanis, I grew up with an image of England as a land of opportunity. Every small village had a tale to tell of how one of their young men had left decades ago and returned from the cold and wet cities as wealthy as a prince. People said it was a place where little attention was paid to whether you were Shia, Sunni, or Wahhabi. Instead I imagined it to be a place where all Pakistanis were equal.

I liked this idea. Having spent all my life as a minority Shia in a majority Sunni city, I was aware that I was different. And given the brutal way in which the Wahhabis were attacking the Shia, there was something about the idea of just being a Pakistani Muslim that I found appealing.

As tensions between Islam and the West increased, so too did Wahhabi attacks on Shia. Around the time that Ami built the new house and we moved in, the frequency and force of their attacks became even more intense, and there were stories of Wahhabi snipers hiding in the minarets of Shia mosques and picking off worshipers as they answered the call to prayer. Though Ami tried to shield me from the worst of it, I overheard enough adults talking, and had plenty of conversations with my friends, to know that Shia needed to be careful.

I was eleven years old when the Wahhabi attacked America, sending the World Trade Center to the ground and lighting the fuse on a conflict that spread all the way to my homeland. I was old enough that September to hear the fear in the conversations that took place in cafés and outside mosques. Some expressed sorrow that Muslims were being targeted for revenge, while others declared that the whole thing was a hoax designed to give President Bush the opportunity to invade Iraq and Afghanistan. For most everyone, however, there was sorrow at the loss of life and fear of what would come next. It was obvious to me and my friends that after a few years of calm, things were about to get dangerous again.

In the end, the threat came not so much from Bush or Blair but from an enemy far closer to home. Our news channels ran a steady wall of coverage of the increasing tensions between us and our neighbor India. Endless reporters, journalists, and people on the street discussed the likelihood of India launching a nuclear attack, though Baba-jan was not one of them.

"They will not start anything," he repeated time after time. "The Indians are too scared of what Bush will do to them if they attack. And besides, the Americans need us to help them fight the Taliban."

It turned out that he was right—the attack never did come—but also that he wasn't quite as sure of himself as he would have people believe. One evening, around the time that the news had given a lot of coverage to the fact that the police were checking for illegal guns, Baba-jan came to see me in my room. In his hands was a large canvas bag, easily big enough to hold a motorbike helmet. From the strain his arms were showing, whatever was in the bag was obviously a lot heavier.

"I need you to hide this for me, Nomi. Don't get rid of it, but just find somewhere for it where nobody else will stumble over it."

He placed the bag on the floor and I walked over for a look. Inside were bullets, hundreds of them, each longer than my biggest finger and a dull gray metal color apart from the brassy tip. I tried to hide my curiosity and excitement, concentrating instead on my plans for hiding it. I knew exactly where I would take it, and as soon as night fell and the house and street were quiet enough, I hauled the bag down the stairs and across the back yard toward the gate that nobody ever used except me when I tended my animals.

With nothing but empty scrubland for hundreds of feet and a clear sky and an almost full moon overhead, I got to work beneath the thorny bush that straddled a disused drain. I had found it a few months before when I had been messing around on my own, and I knew that beneath the metal cover was an area that was bone dry and easily large enough to store the ammo. Just to be sure, I added a few large stones to make a small platform on the bottom of the drain. With the bag finally hidden down there, the cover replaced, and the dirt around the thornbush scuffed up again, I stepped back and congratulated myself and hoped that Baba-jan would never have cause to send me to retrieve the bag.

The real threat to us was not the Indians or the police. The real threat was the same one we always faced: the Wahhabi. When President Musharraf allowed the Americans to come to our country and hunt those Wahhabi who called themselves Taliban, the pressure was felt in places like mine. Even though we were hundreds of miles away from the mountains that separated our two countries, we knew they were among us and their centuries-old vendetta against Shia still burned within them.

Sharib and I were together on the day when we saw for ourselves the full and lethal extent of their hatred of Shia. It was just before the start of summer, not long after my failure and subsequent success on the end-of-year math exam. I was telling my cousin all about it, laughing a little and sharing my relief at not having to repeat the school year. I remember we were waiting to buy some corn at one of my favorite stalls, where it was cooked slowly on the coals by a man who looked as though he had been sitting and tending to his fire since the days of Muhammad himself.

It was a busy street, and the man always did a good trade, so we didn't mind waiting too much. I was watching an old man on the other side as he watered his garden. He was a Shia *zakir* and I asked Sharib if he knew of him.

Sharib was straining to get a better look when a motorbike pulled up outside his house. Two men were riding, both dressed in black. Between them was a gun. As the man on the back raised it to his shoulder, I could tell it was an AK47. The *zakir* had not looked up when the bike stopped, but one of the men must have said something, for I watched the old man suddenly stand up and face them. A fraction of a second later, the gun went off and the old man was down.

Nobody—not Sharib or me, not the old man slowly tending the coals and the corn or any of the other customers waiting, or anyone else on the street—said a thing. We all knew to stay quiet and draw as little attention to ourselves as possible. A hundred eyes watched the bike as it swept around and began to drive off. Many of those eyes also noticed the *zakir* stand up, his hand clutching his side, and start to run out of his garden and into the road. All of us heard the bike's engine drop out, then rev up again, getting louder and louder as it brought the two men back to the house and the stumbling *zakir*. He tried to outrun them, but it was no use. This time they left themselves in no doubt that he was dead.

I was fifteen and had just witnessed my first murder—a shock to my system of privilege and security. For days I found it hard to concentrate, my mind seemingly desperate to replay the final moment of the man's death over and over. I could hear the crack and thud of the bullets in perfect detail, see the way his body twitched at first, then moved only with the force of each round that entered him. And I felt the same hollow ache inside that I felt as I watched the gunmen wheel away for the second time, slower than the first, their eyes scanning the crowd for any sign of resistance.

All these images came back to me at the worst times: when I was trying to sleep, when I was trying to study, when I was trying to pray. Between the flickering images, a disturbing question rose within me: Would I ever be willing to die for my faith as the *zakir* had done?

I had no answer. And my uncertainty filled me with fear and self-doubt.

CHAPTER 5

LEAVING PAKISTAN

Distraction is a powerful tool. The rise in fear and uncertainty about the sincerity of my faith troubled me greatly, and I tried my best to put such concerns from my mind. So during the long summer vacation of 2006, I decided to get to work planning my future. I had just avoided the shame of having to retake the academic year and saw it as the perfect time to begin what I knew would be a long campaign of asking Ami and Baba-jan to buy me a motorbike. All the signs were that their resistance wouldn't last much longer than a few months. I'd started to add more and more detail to the daydreams about what my life as an adult would look like. Lying on my bed, allowing the early days of my vacation to slip past hour by hour, I saw cars and houses and a growing number of *mureed*.

That last part of my vision for my future had just become a whole lot clearer thanks to a random meeting I'd had before the end of term. I was out late one evening, sitting with a friend outside the same café where Ami had beaten the drunk man with her shoe, when my friend tapped me on the arm.

"You see that man there," he said, pointing to a guy a couple of years older. "Do you know him?"

"No."

"You should meet him. He's Asim, and he's a friend of my cousin's. You'd like him."

So we sauntered over, and the three of us got talking. We traded information in the usual way, asking each other what our family name was, where we lived, who our relatives were. Within minutes it was clear that we had a lot in common, so much so that Asim was my cousin on my father's side.

Asim lived in a part of Lahore where I'd never really spent much time, so I suppose it wasn't too surprising we'd never met before. What did surprise me was that he didn't appear to hold any kind of grudge against me for the fact that my mother had divorced his uncle. Yet I still felt a little hesitant about asking him too much about my father.

"You should come with me tomorrow," he said as he prepared to leave. "I want to show you something in the mosque."

The mosque was over in his side of the city, and it was bigger than any other mosque I had been to. I followed him inside, removing my shoes and following other men to the taps where I could wash my hands and say the prayers to complete my purification. I often felt a kind of nervousness whenever I entered a mosque, aware how important it was to do and say the right things—especially as a Sayed. This time those feelings were even stronger. The ceilings were higher than in my own mosque, and where I was used to plain walls and simple tiled floors, the interior of this mosque was spectacular. The walls and ceilings were covered in delicate patterns of blue, gold, and jade, while the floors were highly polished stone that looked as though it cost a small fortune.

Asim took me through to the prayer hall. Instead of seeing a crowd of men kneeling down on their mats, I saw a number of them gathered in one corner of the hall. They were sitting in front of three men, each sitting on an elaborately carved wooden chair. In front were baskets and I watched as the routine played out. One man from the crowd would approach whoever sat in the chair, first placing something— money, I guessed—in the basket. They would talk for a while, then the first man would leave and another would approach.

"When your father dies," whispered Asim, talking about my real father, "you will sit here too. Men will come to you for counsel and prayer."

We left soon after, but the image and the ideas it birthed stayed with me for days. I didn't feel wise yet, but I hoped I would be one day.

Knowing this helped shape my aspirations, which had changed considerably since I was small. As a child I had wanted to be a soldier, but that hope shattered when, a year after I broke my leg mysteriously and there was that business with the *jinn*, I broke it a second time. On this second occasion there was no suspicion of foul play. I was simply a fool who jumped from too high a branch and landed too badly on too hard a patch of earth. And where Ami had been sympathetic before, this time she punched me on the shoulder as I lay on the bed in the clinic. I knew she was mad we'd have to miss our holiday to the mountains that summer, but I also knew her scowls were only put on as an act. She loved me and cared for me, and every day of the three months that I was forced to stay in bed, she sat by my bedside in the evening, talking until I drifted off to sleep.

Even though the second break weakened my leg and curbed my military ambitions, it left me with a blank page on which my dreams of being a businessman had started to be sketched. Like any adolescent boy, I was beginning to discover how good it felt to be making plans for myself.

My reputation at Uncle Faizal's was also good at the start of the summer. I wasn't the best at Tekken, but I was getting better and depending on the time of day and who else was in, I could remain undefeated on the machine for almost an hour.

I was midway through a battle when Ami tapped me on the shoulder. Instinctively I started to apologize, but she stopped me. "I came about Aunt Gulshan," she said, guiding me out to the street. "She is not well."

"What is it?"

"She says it is her kidneys and she might not be able to return to Pakistan again. You need to pray for her, Nomi."

"I will," I said, determining to pray diligently for her, pleading with Allah to be merciful and restore her health.

"You need to pray for something else as well," said Ami. "I want you and Zainab to go to England to see her, and for that you will need a visa. And to get one of them you are going to have to pray even more."

Excitement at the thought of going to England ignited within, but it was to Aunt Gulshan that my mind soon turned. I had so many memories of her to choose from. Her yearly visits were always a highlight for me, and the fact that Ami always placed her *charpai* next to my bed only increased my sense of fascination. When the room was lit by nothing but the moon outside, I would lie awake, perfectly still, and listen as she prayed. Just as she had on that first day when her hand sent raging heat through my leg, Aunt Gulshan prayed in Urdu, the language of the family. And where the prayers that I uttered were taken from a prescribed menu, hers were so varied that I marveled at how anybody could learn so many different words.

Most of all, though, I was fascinated by the silences she left. Often, after some minutes of whispering her words, she would pause. In those moments I would feel my breath grow light within me, as if someone had made the air one hundred times sweeter. I could hear my heart beating, notice new sounds that came from outside the window. In those moments of precious silence, so much noise filled my head. But it was never unsettling, never chaotic. The silence brought with it the most wonderful sense of peace, more delicious than anything I had ever encountered.

It was these memories of my aunt that drove me to pray earnestly for a visa. I couldn't match her passion or sense anything like the mysterious silences that came so often whenever she prayed, but I petitioned Allah for the chance to go and visit.

On Ami's advice, Zainab and I had not mentioned anything about our planned trip to anyone else. We hadn't even discussed it among ourselves, fearful that somebody might overhear us and our plans would vanish overnight. Instead I simply held the hope within me, burying it along with my prayers for Aunt Gulshan's health and a successful visa application. For two weeks I kept it hidden in this way, sometimes forgetting about it for most of the day, at other times devoting whole hours to elaborate imaginings about what life would be like over there. These were hazy images and are hard to describe, but they captivated me all the same.

"You know," said Ami repeatedly whenever she interrupted my daydreams. "England is not like it is on those Bollywood films. The people there will more likely shout at you than stand around and cheer as you dance through the streets."

"I know that," I'd say, convinced that Ami didn't know quite as much as she thought she did about the place.

Applying for a visa required a visit to the British Consulate in Lahore. I expected to find a room full of white men in nice suits sitting behind heavy wooden desks inquiring politely about my aunt. Instead the place appeared to be staffed exclusively by people who looked like me but who carried themselves with a potent air of superiority.

"Not like Bollywood, eh?" said Ami, digging me in the ribs as she, Zainab, and I sat on hard plastic chairs and stared about us at the dirty floor and the line of perspex interview booths. The combination of unsmiling staff and hushed conversations left me feeling nervous, even almost guilty for being there, as if merely asking to visit was a crime. Eventually I was called up to discuss my application, and after a series of questions in Urdu—which I answered just as politely and briefly as Ami had told me to—I was told that my application had been successful.

It turned out that a visit to Uncle Faizal's could be made even better when you had news of an imminent trip to some exotic foreign location to share. On the evening after I returned from the Consulate, as I stood around drinking a soda, people I'd barely spoken to before came up to me, asking me what I was going to be doing in England, and could I bring them back this or that item they wanted. I was sure that I felt just about as grown up and successful as any fifteen-year-old had ever felt.

I was nervous when the day of the flight came and we left for the airport. I was a little kid again, my muscles refusing to rest, my legs twitching all through the journey. I felt better as soon as I was out of the car and pushing a trolley in front of me, and once we were inside and had found the first of what Ami had told me were many security checks, I was impatient to get going.

"Nomi," said Ami as I tried to see through the security doors to the crowd of people on the other side. "Listen to me." Her tug on my arm pulled my attention back to her. Her eyes compelled me to stare back into them, and I couldn't have broken the gaze even if I'd wanted to. "Your aunt is a bit different. Be careful."

I wasn't entirely sure what she meant. Of course I knew there was something special about Aunt Gulshan. I knew that her prayers were different from mine, that she always wore sunglasses and that her health was not good. But something about the way Ami looked at me told me there was more to it than that. Despite all that, I was too wired and ready to go to give it much thought. "Yes, Ami, I know," I said before giving her a kiss goodbye and leading Zainab through the doors ahead.

My enthusiasm evaporated with the starting of the engines. Takeoff turned me into a wreck of nerves and raw fear, while every noise and jolt on the nine-hour flight sent me deeper into my seat. Zainab was able to eat and sleep and watch movies, but all I could do was pray that the wings would stay on long enough for us to reach land in one piece.

I felt worse when I was handed a landing card to fill in. My English was good enough to count to ten and list a few of their best cricket and soccer players, but the words on the card made zero sense to me. I was grateful that Zainab was sixteen at the time, a whole year older than me and clearly a good deal more diligent as a student.

By the time the flight was coming to an end, the lack of sleep caught up with me. I managed to lock myself in the toilet where I felt safe enough to close my eyes and allow my head to grow heavy and

thoughts to drift, but a loud knock and a stern word from an atten-
dant sent me back to my seat. Through the windows I could see land,
painted green and gray by some giant's hand. I shrank back into my
seat, pulled my belt tighter than it had been before, and closed my eyes.
We'd either crash and be hurled to our deaths or make it down alive. I
honestly had no idea which outcome was more likely.

CHAPTER 6

AN INFIDEL IN
THE FAMILY

I had little idea what to expect when we arrived at Heathrow, but the cold air seemed about right. Ami had helped me pack and I was glad she'd put some extra clothes in my carry-on bag, for even though it was summer in England, it felt like winter to me.

Zainab and I let ourselves get caught up in the surging tide of people as it flowed out from the plane and deeper into the airport. From other doorways more passengers flowed, all taking their place in the human river. There was a system in play, and it was easy to spot: young men in suits wove their way artfully between people, moving further up the pack while old people waited silently at the side. Back home the elderly would have been treated with more respect, I was sure of that.

Around every corner was another long, wide corridor of glass walls and low ceilings. At times I wondered whether our walk was ever going to end, but for Zainab's sake I hid my uncertainty and strode on with all the confidence I could summon.

We turned a final corner, entered a large hall, and were brought to a halt as the crowd slowly separated itself off into different lines. I looked about me, trying to work out where we should go. "Over here," said Zainab, marching on ahead toward a large knot of people at the far end of the hall.

It must have taken an hour for us to make it toward the front of the line. After a long flight my legs were stiff and tired, and all that shuffling along, inch by inch, only made them feel worse. Still, Zainab and I used the time to go over our plan. As soon as we reached the immigration desk, we agreed that we would step up together, I would make our introduction, and Zainab would continue with the explanation of why we were there.

The plan failed at the first. The balding man behind the desk nodded at us, we approached, and I blurted out my greeting so quickly that he just blinked at us and held out his hand for our passports and paperwork, a disinterested expression on his face.

"How long are you staying here?"

"Six weeks," I said, happy that the foreign words came out clearly. When he asked why we had come to England, I nudged Zainab forward, but she was mute with fear so it was up to me to stumble through the rest of the interview.

I told him about Aunt Gulshan, how she was ill. I forgot the English word for "kidneys" but remembered to show him our return tickets.

He looked at me carefully. "If your aunt is sick, how is she going to be able to look after you and your sister?"

Again, I struggled to find the words, but somehow I managed to tell him that Aunt Gulshan had someone whose job it was to look after her at home.

"You mean a carer?"

"Yes," I said, hoping that whatever a *carer* was it would be the right thing to persuade him to let us in. "I have this as well," I said, handing over the piece of paper on which Ami had written Aunt Gulshan's phone number. The man picked it up, shrugged, and said, "Wait here." Zainab and I watched him pick up our passports along with the paper and pass through a door at the end of the hall. The crowd had thinned considerably by this time, and a strange feeling settled on us both as we waited. I didn't like the way I suddenly felt alone.

Ten minutes later the man returned. "I spoke to your aunt and she says she's outside waiting for you." With that, he stamped our passports and handed them back to us. "Enjoy your stay."

Aunt Gulshan was right where he said she would be. It had been a couple of years since she had visited us in Pakistan, and the sight of her in a wheelchair troubled me, but the sense of relief at arriving safe by her side was stronger.

Next to her was a short lady dressed in typical Hindu clothing. "This is Emily," said Aunt Gulshan and we shook hands.

"I've heard a lot about you," said Emily, giving me a quick half smile before turning and embracing Zainab. Though she looked and dressed like an Indian, her accent sounded just like that of the English people I'd heard on TV. Our greetings over, Emily led the way, pushing my aunt ahead of her while Zainab and I followed close behind. There was no skipping through the airport from me this time. I was far too in awe of everything.

It was the cars that impressed me the most. I had been used to seeing a few nice ones around Lahore, but this was something else. As we made our way through the parking lot, I spotted dozens of high-end vehicles of the sort of quality that would have drawn an instant crowd back home. Yet here the BMWs, Mercedes, and even Porsches were wedged in side by side with lesser makes, squeezed together like they were cattle at a market. Back home nobody would dare park so close to one of these exotic imports. I wondered how many other rules I was going to encounter that were different over here.

Aunt Gulshan's car was not one of the high-end ones, but it was nice enough. Emily edged it out of the lot and away from the airport. Zainab's eyes were just as wide as mine as we passed under giant billboards and through brightly lit tunnels. I was still looking at the cars, straining my neck to see a gleaming Jaguar as it sailed by.

At some point in the hour-long journey out to my aunt's home in Oxford, we pulled into a supermarket for groceries. I had never seen such a place. I walked through the electric doors into a blast of cold air and felt as though I'd wandered into some giant's kingdom. Aunt Gulshan must have noticed me, for she prodded me gently in the arm and said, "It is not like home, is it?"

"No," I murmured. "And this is just one shop? It is as big as a whole mall back home."

Emily laughed. "You will find a lot of things are different over here."

I didn't understand her laughing like that, but I shrugged it off and went back to staring down the endless aisles and up at the ceiling that looked far more impressive than the one in the airport. Zainab and I trailed on behind Emily as she spun my aunt across the polished floors. There were bananas three times the size they were back home and baskets full of vegetables that looked as though every single one had already been washed free of mud. I wondered how many people they needed to have working in the back of the store to get everything in such immaculate condition.

As we rounded one corner, I let out a shout and grabbed Zainab by the shoulders.

"Close your eyes, sister!" I said. "Look away!" Just a few feet ahead of us was a young couple embracing and kissing, right there in front of row upon row of different breads. Neither Zainab nor I had ever seen Ami and Baba-jan holding hands while we were at home, and such a display of affection would never take place in public in Pakistan. Aunt Gulshan was reading a packet and didn't seem to have noticed anything, but I looked up to see Emily laughing once more. "So many things are different," she said.

Over the coming days, Emily made it clear that Aunt Gulshan was not well and explained that she needed regular trips to the hospital. But contrary to what I had thought when we first heard about her, Aunt Gulshan did not appear to be about to die at any moment. In fact, she was well enough to be asking endless questions about life back home, inquiring about relatives I could barely remember. I enjoyed sitting with her, though. Just hearing her voice reminded me of all the times I'd listened to her praying.

I knew nothing about Oxford but took an instant liking to the city all the same. In some ways it reminded me of home. There was something familiar and comforting about the way it became so crowded during the day, with people skipping on and off the teeming sidewalks, weaving in and out of traffic. The buildings were captivating too, with some of the larger ones stretching out like a tiger lying in the afternoon sun. I wondered whether some of the British architects who helped create Lahore were thinking of these famous colleges when they started their sketches. It reminded me of how powerful the United Kingdom was once.

I saw beggars and street traders, familiar sights at home as well, but it was the number of people from my homeland that really held my attention. There were some streets in the city where every other voice I heard was speaking Urdu or Punjabi. The accents came from all over the country—from snowy mountains in the north to sweltering coastal cities in the south—but every single one reminded me that even though home was thousands of miles away, it really wasn't all that far.

Some things continued to shock me, however. The public displays of affection always made me stop and check that Zainab's eyes were averted, and the clothes that some girls wore—little more than their underwear in some cases—had me closing my own eyes and trying to get my mind to think of something else.

Less shocking, and far safer for me to look at, were the stores that sold electronics. I got a buzz just from standing in front of them and looking at all the items for sale. Phones and laptops and TVs were status symbols back home, and stores with stocks like these would typically only ever be found in cities and big towns. They would have gun-toting security guards out front, and they would have kept undesirable customers out. Yet in Oxford anyone could walk into these stores and take a look. I happily joined with the crowds as they stared, glassy-eyed, at the ranks of flashing screens on display.

When Zainab and I first accompanied Aunt Gulshan on her visit to the hospital, I was left with much the same feeling. There was more medical equipment in that one room than I had seen in any hospital back in Pakistan, and I knew my aunt was lucky to be receiving such care. And even though the doctors who darted in and out of her room exhaled that same sense of calm control and total confidence that they did back home, it seemed obvious to me that in Pakistan someone with Aunt Gulshan's condition would be lucky to make it out alive.

As well as a large Pakistani community that seemed to live mainly along the Cowley Road, one of the main roads into the city, Oxford was full of other nationalities. Packs of students from all over the world crowded the sidewalks outside the colleges, shops, and museums. Even away from the city center, it was possible to hear so many different languages being spoken that at times I wondered where all the English people had gone to. For me, a teenage boy who'd never seen a Chinese or black person before, every trip outside Aunt Gulshan's terraced house was yet another reminder of how far I was from home.

I found it hard not to stare at people at first, and I would happily accompany Emily on any outing to the supermarket that she planned, no matter how dull she said it would be. Before I left Pakistan, Baba-jan had bought a video camera, and on the morning Zainab and I flew out, he handed it over to me with great care. He had given me strict instructions both to fully document my trip and to keep the video camera safe, and my shopping expeditions with Emily appeared to me to be the perfect opportunity to document English life in full detail. But when a shop worker with a face as sour as any I had ever encountered swore at me for filming her at work, I decided that complying with both of Baba-jan's wishes was an impossible task and chose to leave the camera at home from then on.

I got so accustomed to staring at people that I often forgot I was doing it, but everywhere I looked there was another example of how strangely familiar yet also foreign this world was to me. I watched men spilling out of mosques after Friday prayers and saw women argue with their husbands in the middle of a shopping mall. I saw boys playing cricket near billboards depicting naked women. Beggars lay draped on the ground outside bookshops and police officers chatted with them as if they were old friends. The familiar and the foreign existed side by side.

After a week of being in Oxford, I decided I wanted to do more than just stare. I wanted to talk to people.

Not far from Aunt Gulshan's house was a basketball court set at the edge of a large park. I had already filmed people playing there, and I figured it would be as good a place as any for me to find someone who would be willing to talk to me. Leaving Zainab at home preparing food with Emily and Aunt Gulshan, I walked to the court one afternoon when the sun was just starting to get a little warm.

Three boys, all I guessed a little older than me, were playing. "Hello," I said as I approached the court. "I would like to play basketball with you."

The boys didn't appear to have heard me, so I walked a little closer to the end where they were gathered and tried again.

"Hello," I said. "My name is Ali Husnain. May I join you?"

Two of the boys stared blankly back at me, while the third and tallest of them mumbled something I couldn't quite understand.

"Could you repeat that, please?" I said, hoping to catch his words a second time. I was trying my best to be confident like I would have been back at Uncle Faizal's, but when the other two started laughing, I knew they were just playing with me.

I headed back home, ignoring their laughter that carried on far longer than was natural. *I suppose there are* umti *everywhere,* I thought to myself.

I wasn't ready to give up and decided to try again the next day. I liked the park and was sure that if the weather was fine some other day, there was one other way I could try to meet people.

The sun was just as bright the next day, so as soon as Aunt Gulshan, Emily, and Zainab started preparing food again, I told them I was going back out for an hour and made my way through the maze of streets lined with parked cars. Once I was back at the park, I didn't even bother looking at who was playing on the basketball court. Instead I made my way to a bench beside the concrete path that ran around the park's edge. I'd spent enough time with my video camera here to know it wouldn't be long before a jogger came by, and when they did, I would put my plan into action.

While I had been watching people go about their lives in Oxford, I had noticed that people rarely talked to each other, unless they were friends in the first place. Back home I knew I could talk to anyone; there were no invisible walls behind which people hid. But here it was different. Not that I was surprised, because Ami had warned me before I left. "The English are good, trustworthy people," she had said. "But they spend a lot of time thinking that everyone else around them is *umti*."

I had remembered her words as I walked away from the basketball court, and it helped to take almost all the sting out of the boys' rudeness. But I'd also remembered something else. While most people had their invisible walls up around them, keeping strangers away, there were times when I had seen and heard people approach someone on the street and start up a conversation. It was just a matter of knowing the right thing to say.

Until I arrived in England, I had never seen anyone out jogging before. Of course I had seen plenty of people running, but mostly they were either being chased by the police or trying to escape a roadside bomb laid by the Wahhabi. I had no idea running could be a leisure activity, but as I'd observed the joggers plodding around the park, it struck me that it looked kind of fun.

I didn't have to wait long. Within a couple of minutes a heavy man about Baba-jan's age with a dog on a long lead went past. I wasn't sure whether the dog was benefiting from the exercise or the man was benefiting from being pulled along by the dog, but I decided to strike. When he had gone a few feet past me, I jumped up and followed. His pace was slow, and I fell in behind him for a few strides before accelerating and running alongside him.

"Hello," I said to the jogger as we bumped along the path together.

Either he had not seen or heard me or I had picked someone with a thicker wall than others. So I decided to use the line that I was absolutely sure would work.

"What is the time?"

That, at least, got his attention. He looked at me and stumbled a little before taking a sharp right turn away from me and across the grass.

I did not want to be defeated for a second day, so I walked back to my bench and waited for another jogger to approach. This time it was a woman, and it took a little more effort from me to keep up with her. But the result was the same, with my polite request eliciting nothing more than a confused look and a sudden burst of speed.

I must have spent almost an hour like this, chasing people and asking them for the time. Some of them looked at their watches and told me it was four-something, but the conversation never went any further.

I was just about to give up when a Chinese guy—the first I had seen that day—ran past. I got up from my bench and made one last dash. "What is the time?"

He stopped, scrunched up his face, and said a word I didn't recognize but which I took to be friendly enough. "What is the time?" I asked again, tapping my wrist.

This time he understood and shrugged, showing me that he had no watch on. But then he started talking to me, babbling on in what must have been Chinese. We returned to the bench and sat there for a few minutes, him speaking in Chinese, me switching between English and Urdu. I didn't understand a word he said, and I'm sure he was just as confused, but in that one moment I felt a small thrill of victory.

I was telling Emily about this the next day as we drove to the supermarket. The roads were busy and I could tell she was only half listening to me. When a car whipped out in front of us abruptly, causing Emily to hit the brakes hard, she cursed a little. This surprised me. She wore a cross around her neck, and though I didn't know much about Christianity, it struck me as odd.

I went back to my story and soon was telling Emily about what life was like back home. "What happened on the basketball court would never happen to me at home. Being a Shah means that we are respected, that people treat us well and would not think to be rude in any way."

"That doesn't count for anything over here, though, does it?" she said.

I thought about it. She was right, but I didn't mind too much. Life at home was good and I wasn't troubled by my temporary decline in status here in England. More than all the material possessions, the security and the reputation, I knew that life was secure, solid. When I got back home to Pakistan, I would be ready to start my ascent into adulthood.

"I think I'm learning things here," I said. "I am learning about what it feels like to be disrespected and unimportant. I don't really think about it much at home, but being *umti*, like the Christians who run my school, must be hard."

Emily drove on in silence for a while, but I could tell that she was about to speak. Her hands were tight on the wheel and her eyes looked ahead intensely. Eventually she spoke. "You should be careful what you say about Christians. Your aunt is one of them."

I didn't fully understand her words at first. We drove a while longer, Emily's words filling the silence in the car like a cloud of confusion. Calling Aunt Gulshan a Christian—a *kafir*—was such a strange thing to say that I wondered whether I had properly understood Emily. The more I thought about it, the more I believed that what she had meant was that Aunt Gulshan had lived in England for so long it was as if she were *umti* herself.

Though I had never personally known anyone who had turned their back on Islam and become apostate, I'd heard enough stories to know that choosing to become a *kafir* was a mistake that could easily cost you your life.

I couldn't imagine Aunt Gulshan doing such a thing. Sure, she was a little unusual, just as Ami had reminded me at the airport, but there was no way I could imagine Emily's comment to be true. If anything, it helped explain some of that unusual behavior—like the way she prayed and the fact that she rarely wore any kind of head covering. She had been away so long that she had become Westernized. *That is what Emily meant,* I told myself. *That and nothing more.*

A few minutes farther down the road, Emily pulled into the supermarket. "I wasn't lying," she said as she turned off the engine and fixed her eyes on me. "Your aunt really is a Christian."

I looked hard at her, trying to work out whether she might be trying to tease me. "She's written a book about it as well. You can see for yourself when we get home." With that, she climbed out of the car and marched off across the parking lot toward the giant glass doors and the strange world beyond them.

See for myself? I thought. If Aunt Gulshan truly was a Christian, then *she* was the one who needed to see things clearly again.

CHAPTER 7

"COME BACK TO ISLAM"

When I first tried to bring up the subject of my aunt's book, she pretended not to hear me. This happened twice, then three times. Eventually, a few days after Emily and I visited the supermarket, I decided I needed to be more direct. "Aunt Gulshan," I said again as she sat at the table after we had finished eating breakfast, "Emily told me that you have written a book. I would like to read it, please."

She stared silently at the table in front of her for some time, not acknowledging my words. I was beginning to wonder whether Emily had played a trick on me when Aunt Gulshan spoke. "I have written a book, but it is not the type of book that you would want to read." The silence that followed took me right back to the day when I first met her as I lay down, a sharp pain carving its way through my leg. I fought the urge to look away.

"I think I would like to try, though," I said before taking a risk and speaking again. "Perhaps it will help me to understand . . ." I paused, not deliberately leaving the sentence unfinished, but just incapable of finishing it myself.

Aunt Gulshan looked back at her hands. She made a noise like she was clearing her throat but fell silent again. I was confused by the whole thing, surprised that she appeared to be finding it so hard to hand over a book that she herself had written.

"Is there anything about me in it?" I asked.

"What?"

"Am I in the book?"

Her expression lightened. Was she amused? "No, Ali, it was written before you were born."

Zainab came in and the conversation ended. But when I went up to my room later that morning, I found on my covers a small paperback. I picked it up and carefully examined it. A pair of hazel-colored eyes framed by a *niqab* stared out at me from the cover. *The Torn Veil*, I read. I wasn't used to seeing Aunt Gulshan's name written down in English, but there it was, Gulshan Esther. Seeing her name in print made me smile.

For the next few hours, I lay on my foldaway bed in the guest room in the afternoon sun, turning page after page. I felt as though I was thousands of miles away, back in Pakistan.

My English wasn't good enough for me to be able to understand every word, but as I started the first page I saw enough to set my heart beating a little faster. I read about her family back in Pakistan—also named Shah—and about her home in the town of Jhang. And while I had never met her brothers or sisters and had never visited the family home she described, I felt a thrill knowing that these people she mentioned were related to me as well.

What amazed me the most, however, were the descriptions of her health back when she was a child. I had long known that Aunt Gulshan had not been well, and the problem with her kidneys was the latest in a long line of health problems that Ami had informed us about over the years. But according to the book, when she was my age Aunt Gulshan's physical condition was far worse than it was now. I read about her crippled left side, how she was unable to wash, feed, or walk because of a terrible, paralyzing disease that had struck when she was just six months old. I had to go back over the passage a number of times to make sure I was reading it correctly, but each time my mind created the same picture of a weak, vulnerable girl who—were it not for her status as a Shah—most likely would have been pushed away and ignored by everyone. Her health was poor again now, but my memories of her when she visited us in Pakistan were of a different, stronger woman. She had not been in a wheelchair when she visited us then. Something had changed.

I skimmed on, reading about her hopes that she would be healed when she made *hajj*, the sacred pilgrimage to Mecca. Yet her leg and arm remained just as weak when she left, and I found myself feeling sorry for her. Never in my life had I considered Aunt Gulshan someone who needed my pity. She was always so strong, a tiger of a woman who never showed any fear at all. But this little girl I was reading about was different, as if she were someone else entirely.

I already knew that her mother had died when Aunt Gulshan was young, so reading about the death of her father saddened me further. New detail was added to my mental picture of a young girl with a body that could not support itself; I saw her crippled by sorrow as well, brought down to a place so low that I wondered how on earth she ever managed to survive.

It was on page 58 that everything changed. Aunt Gulshan was in her room one night, quietly praying. At first I didn't understand the significance of this, but on reading the passage again I saw that she was praying not to Allah, but to Jesus—a prophet occasionally mentioned in the Qur'an. She was praying to him for healing when the room filled with light and he appeared right there in front of her, along with twelve other men. Jesus spoke, telling her to get up. As far as I could tell Aunt Gulshan hadn't ever been able to do that, but in that room in the middle of the night, she stood for the first time in nineteen years. Jesus, the man who only briefly appears in the Qur'an, then taught her a prayer, made her clothes turn pure white, and told her to tell other people about him.

I put down the book and looked up. For a brief moment I felt surprised to find myself in Oxford and not back in Pakistan in a low-ceilinged room that was filled with light. My breath had grown light within me, the air suddenly sweetened, and I was reminded once more of what it felt like to be a boy in those moments when I would sit in the silence that filled the room when Aunt Gulshan prayed in the bed next to mine.

I closed my eyes and returned to the room in which Aunt Gulshan stood, her body miraculously healed. The scenario was captivating, but dangerous.

I read how the news of Aunt Gulshan's healing was greeted well initially but how it eventually resulted in her being forced to leave the family. Aunt Gulshan met Christians, but they did not show her the kind of respect that a Shah deserved. There was an amazing story about her sister dying, only to come back to life once Aunt Gulshan prayed for her. Then she was tricked and imprisoned, and her brothers contemplated murdering her. It was too much to take in, and even on the last page there was a story about her brother having a heart attack, dying, and seeing hell in front of him before Jesus appeared and he begged the prophet to help him the same way he had helped Aunt Gulshan. So he woke up and spent eight hours sitting in the morgue, waiting for someone to come in the next morning and open up.

It was dark when I finished the book. Though I could hear Zainab and Emily moving about downstairs and preparing for our evening meal, but I was not ready to join them. I needed to stay where I was. I needed to think.

A part of me had been amazed by what I read in the book. Though I had been asked many times to pray for somebody's healing, I had always assumed my prayers wouldn't be answered until that person reached the afterlife. I knew Allah had the power to heal, but I had never heard of anything as dramatic as Aunt Gulshan's miraculous healing. So I was intrigued and amazed.

But that was not all I was feeling.

I thought about the sorrow of her family and the dishonor she brought upon them. I thought about what her father would have said to know that his daughter brought such joy to the family and then so much pain. I thought about the words Ami had spoken to me at the airport, reminding me that Aunt Gulshan was unusual. Was this what she meant?

Mostly, though, I thought about the fact that Aunt Gulshan was a *kafir*. She was apostate. She had committed an unforgivable sin and brought shame upon our family. It was hard to take in.

Eventually I went down to eat, though I wasn't hungry. I sat quietly through the meal, barely eating my rice. When Emily and Zainab left, it was Aunt Gulshan who spoke first.

"You read my book?"

"Yes."

She paused. "I told you it was not the type of book that you would want to read."

A hundred different questions shot like sparks in my mind. Some were born of fascination with what had happened to her, but many more were born of my anger. I chose my words carefully.

"You wrote that the man Jesus made your *shalwar kameez* white and that he told you to keep it. Where is it? Can I see it?"

"No," she said. "I do not have it." I scrunched up my face and she laughed. "This all happened long before you were born, Ali, and all clothes wear out eventually." She paused again, looking at me in a way that reminded me of how I felt whenever Ami was about to tell me off. "The real miracles are the ones that never fade."

I was confused by her response, but felt a little bolder too. So I decided to say the thought that had been playing throughout my head all during the meal. "Did you just decide to tell people that you had become a *k . . .*" I caught myself. I didn't want to offend her. ". . . a Christian because you wanted to live in England?" I sat back and waited for her to respond, convinced that if this was like a game of Tekken at Uncle Faizal's, I had just delivered a knockout kick that guaranteed me victory.

Aunt Gulshan just smiled. "Husnain-ji," she said, "if I had wanted to come to England, there would have been a thousand easier ways to do so."

With that, she called for Emily and the conversation ended.

The next few days passed much like all the others, with Zainab and me accompanying Emily and Aunt Gulshan on trips to the hospital for her dialysis. Between visits to the supermarket, Aunt Gulshan's daytime naps, and my trips to the park where I continued my attempts to engage people in conversation, there weren't many opportunities to continue the discussion of Aunt Gulshan's rejection of Islam. So I decided to pray instead. I asked Allah to use me to help bring Aunt Gulshan back to Islam, rejecting all this nonsense about Jesus and giving true credit for her healing to Allah.

I wondered whether Ami knew this might happen, even whether she had intended for Zainab and me to try to bring our aunt back to Islam. Ami had packed in my bag a prayer mat, and though I hadn't used it much in the first week of my trip, once I read Aunt Gulshan's book I took my duties as a good Muslim more seriously. At least once each day I unrolled it and placed it on the thin strip of floor at the side of my bed, which just happened to be facing Mecca. And when I finished praying I liked to imagine what the reaction would be at home when they heard the news that Aunt Gulshan had finally stopped all this Christian nonsense and pledged once more her devotion to Allah.

"Tonight some of my friends from church are visiting," she said one afternoon.

"Why?" I asked, a little too aggressively, for my question attracted a stern stare from both Zainab and Emily.

"They come here every month and we pray, read the Bible, and talk. You can come too if you like."

Was this a trick? Nothing about her expression suggested it, and Emily looked happy enough. "Yes," I said. "I will come."

I spent the afternoon trying to imagine what the evening would be like, but my only comparisons were the *majlis* we held at home. On those occasions hundreds of people gathered outside, the police closed the roads, and the preaching lasted all day. I couldn't imagine how more than a few people could fit into Aunt Gulshan's main room downstairs.

It turned out that this was about the only thing I guessed correctly about the evening. Nine people arrived in all and talked quietly among themselves in pairs and threes while they waited for the meeting to start.

I was waiting in the kitchen, watching Zainab prepare the drinks, when Aunt Gulshan invited me in. "This is Ali," she said. "From Pakistan."

That won me a lot of smiles and warm greetings. Some people asked me how I liked England and whether I was bothered by the cold. Someone else asked me if I had been to Oxford before and another asked me what church I went to at home.

"Oh no," said Aunt Gulshan. "Ali does not go to church. He is a Muslim."

At that the smiles became a little wider and the polite conversation ended. The small woman seated next to me shifted in her seat and started searching awkwardly in her bag.

The meeting progressed and I tried to understand the pattern. It was so very different from anything I had been to before. First, it was a mixed group, and the women were not separated from the men. They were free to talk as well, which the woman next to me did a lot more than anyone else. Nobody seemed to be in charge, apart perhaps from a gentle-looking man with a slow, soft voice who at various points encouraged people to open their Bibles and consider various questions that he read from a sheet.

I had seen Bibles before, or at least I thought I had. But I was shocked to discover that they were available in English. The way the Christians disrespected them was an even greater shock, though. Some people held theirs as if it was any other book, while one man even placed his on the floor. I had never seen anyone treat a holy book in this way. *Perhaps it is not so holy after all*, I thought.

I thought back to my time at home and the door that Ami had me leave open so she could check that the *mullahs* weren't doing anything they shouldn't have been doing with us children. I remembered how I felt frustrated with them when they wouldn't answer my questions.

In many ways, this was different. Everybody who wanted to was able to speak, and no one person taught the others. But I had a whole mountain of questions building up inside me, and it was getting difficult for me to contain them for much longer.

They were talking about someone I had never heard of before. He was called Paul, and as far as I could tell at the time, he had been through some experiences similar to those Aunt Gulshan had faced. He had been a powerful figure, a man with influence, but once he decided to become what they called "a follower of Christ," he became *umti*—becoming blind, getting ill, and ending up in prison. None of what I heard about him made me want to follow either him, the prophet Jesus, or my aunt.

When the woman next to me started talking about how Jesus had healed her of a bad back, I finally had enough.

"How do you know it was Jesus who healed you?" I asked. Though my own thoughts had been screaming inside my head since the start of the meeting, this was the first time I had spoken out loud. The room fell silent and everybody looked at me. The woman shifted a little in her seat.

"I know that it was Jesus," she said. "I felt his touch. I saw his face."

That sounded ridiculous to me. It was one thing to claim to be able to see Jesus, but to feel him too? What kind of *jinn* was this? I snorted and looked at her in disbelief. "Are you sure that it was him? What does Jesus look like? What did it feel like? Can you really be sure that you saw the face of God?"

"You know, Ali," said the man with the questions on the piece of paper, "God is our Father. You don't need to be scared of him. He loves you and is calling you to him."

At this I laughed out loud. It was too much. "You know, we have many, many miracles in Islam, and this prophet Jesus was not the only one who rose from the dead. Did you know that?"

Silence.

These people were absurd, and it felt good to expose them. I wondered what Sharib would say if he could see me, or his father or Baba-jan. Surely they would laugh and clap me on the shoulder when they heard how I visited England and argued with the *kafir* like this.

"I do not believe that this prophet Jesus was the son of God, and you cannot persuade me to believe anything other than that. You are all mistaken on this, just like my aunt."

"Chop!" shouted my aunt, commanding me to stop immediately, using the kind of word and the tone of voice that I had not heard since I was a small boy causing chaos in my grandmother's house. I knew instantly that I had gone too far. Still speaking Urdu, she told me I was rude and should go to my room immediately.

All the air drained from me that instant and I lifted myself from my chair, my eyes fixed on the floor, and left the room as quickly as I could. Upstairs I felt the sense of embarrassment and shame give way to anger. How could she have decided to leave Islam for *this*? It made no sense. Did she not think about how it would bring dishonor to her family? Had she not considered what damage she was causing?

I was still angry when she came to my room later, after I had heard the guests leave. She was calm, much calmer than me. "You should come back to Islam," I spat as she stood in my doorway.

"It is not as simple as that," she said. "You are too young to understand."

That did not help my anger. "I am old enough to know that you have chosen to become a *kafir*, that you have committed the unforgivable sin. Do you remember what the Qur'an says about people who commit *kabira* like that? It says that it is like being a rapist."

Aunt Gulshan just looked at me, her face neither angry nor happy.

She looked tired. "I know," she said. "I have not forgotten about any of that."

She said good night soon after that and left me in my room. I lay back in the dark and wondered what Uncle Haafiz would have said to Aunt Gulshan. Surely he would have been able to find the words, tell some epic story, that would have changed her mind.

I thought about my family at home and wondered how much of this Ami and Baba-jan knew. Did they know about the book? Did they know about the fact that she was telling the world that Jesus had healed her?

And I thought about what would happen if she came back to Pakistan again. If Ami and Baba-jan knew, then perhaps others did too. What would happen to us if people started to gossip about our having a *kafir* in the family? There was no scenario I could imagine that didn't end badly for us.

So I decided I had to do two things. I had to help bring Aunt Gulshan back to Islam. To do this meant finding out what it was about Jesus that made her change in the first place. Why did she start praying to him? If I could understand that, then maybe I could help put things right for her again.

If I failed in that, I had another task ahead of me, one that was harder. I had to keep all of this a secret. Nobody could know what was going on.

CHAPTER 8

JESUS, ONLY JESUS

I saw Aunt Gulshan differently now.

In her book she had described a moment when her brothers discussed killing her, saying that a Sharia court would support them. I played this scene over in my mind many times. Had I been there with her brothers, would I have joined them in their threats? Why did they decide not to kill her? Why did Ami send me here in the first place, knowing that Aunt Gulshan had been such a controversial figure at home?

Pushing her along hospital corridors in her wheelchair as Zainab and I escorted her to routine kidney dialysis sessions, I could never quite decide whether I thought she deserved to die, but I was convinced that my aunt had caused a good deal of shame and sorrow. In rejecting Islam she didn't just turn her back on Allah, but on the whole family. She had rejected the very people who were her flesh and blood.

Part of me felt bad about what I'd said and how I'd behaved. She had been generous to me throughout my time with her in Oxford, and I knew that I had been wrong to disrespect her like that. Had we been back in Pakistan, the adults in the room would have scrambled to their feet and lined up to beat me for my insolence. But then again, had we been in Pakistan and Aunt Gulshan was choosing to associate publicly with these *umti* Christians, then there was no way that I, a good Shia Muslim and a Sayed, would have been staying in her house.

Emily and Aunt Gulshan continued to take us to the park, to

hospital visits, to shopping centers, and it was days before the subject of religion came up again. But when it did, it was Aunt Gulshan who brought it up.

I was sitting downstairs, watching soccer on TV, when she came into the room and sat down next to me.

"It was not easy for me to leave Pakistan," she said quietly. "But I had no choice. I knew that I had inflicted a wound on my family, and leaving the country was the only way that I could think of to lessen their shame."

"That was not the only thing you could do," I said. "You could come back to Islam."

"No, Ali. I could not do that."

"But you are a Sayed. You are a descendant of Muhammad. You come from a good family and are respected and honored by people. Why would you throw all that away to become . . ." I thought carefully about my words, treading more softly this time, not wanting to offend her like I did before, but Aunt Gulshan carried on for me.

"To become a *kafir*?" Her voice was quiet, almost weak, and she looked sadder than I had ever seen her. "I am not what I was anymore. I have the name Sayed, but all of that is gone now. I cannot return." We both stared at the television, neither of us caring about or understanding much of what was going on.

We sat like that for some minutes. To me her sadness was a sign that there might be some hope. If she missed home, I assumed, then perhaps there was a chance she would be willing to see sense and begin to put all this Christian nonsense behind her.

Aunt Gulshan broke the silence. "Would you like to come with me to church tomorrow?"

At first I wanted to scrunch up my face and tell her no, I did not want to go with her to a place so full of *kafir* and *umti*. But as I paused and thought, I wondered whether it might not be such a bad idea after all. If Aunt Gulshan was beginning to regret all that she had left behind, then why would I pass up the opportunity to see what she had chosen? It could be the perfect occasion to help her see just how foolish her choice had been.

I will admit that I was feeling confident as we prepared to go to church. From my experience at the Bible study, Christian meetings had none of the excitement or energy about them that Muslim meetings did. They were quiet affairs, unimpressive. Just like the Christians themselves.

The church was close to Aunt Gulshan's house, and I followed behind one Sunday morning as Emily pushed the wheelchair along the sidewalk. I had not mentioned any of my thoughts about Aunt Gulshan's beliefs to Zainab, and as far as I knew, she had remained at home thinking that the three of us had simply gone out for a walk.

As soon as I stepped off the street and into the church, I sensed how different it was from a mosque. I was not impressed. All my life I had attended mosques, and despite this regularity, I knew they were special places. Wide courtyards big enough for crowds to gather within, white pillars, domed ceilings—these were sacred spaces. One did not enter them without dressing properly, without taking off your shoes in an act of reverence. Hands would be washed and prayers said, and any man attending would be ready to concentrate fully on the prayers as they were called out by the gathered crowd. Mosques were like a courtroom, a university library, or a hospital operating theater. Bigger things were going on within the walls than a mere man could hope to comprehend.

The church, on the other hand, looked as though it was apologizing for being there. It was squeezed in between two other buildings and was made of gray stone. Inside, the atmosphere was even worse, with children running around, people standing and chatting and laughing as if they were waiting for a waiter to come and show them to their table, and a group of musicians playing at the front as if it was a common party.

I followed Emily as she guided Aunt Gulshan to a seat at the front. I knew there would be no separation of the sexes in a church, but I still did not approve. Looking around at all these people wearing their casual clothes, carrying on their own lively conversations, I was bothered by just how much chaos there was in the building. The noise was shocking, and the sight of so many people handling their Bibles with such disrespect—yanking them out of their bags, placing them on the floor beneath their chairs—made me feel sad.

But a confidence began to grow within me too. *How could she give up Islam for this?* I asked myself. *She must have been brainwashed by them. All I have to do is help to clear her eyes.*

My confidence took a knock when, looking about the room, my eyes suddenly locked on those of the woman I had been rude to back at the Bible study. Strangely, she smiled at me as if it had never happened, as if she were even *happy* to see me. Quickly I looked down, remembering the blaze of anger on Aunt Gulshan's face as she sent me up to my room that day.

A man in his twenties sat down next to me. He smiled and said hello, but before we could have a conversation, the room fell silent and the same soft-spoken man who had led the Bible study stood up at the front of the church and started the meeting.

Everybody stood up from their chairs and joined in a song. The words were projected onto a screen at the front, and though I could not read them fast enough, I was able to look around and get a sense of what the song was about. Back home whenever there was singing in a mosque, it was usually done by just one person, often the *zakir*. Uncle Haafiz was the best I had ever heard, and his voice rose and fell like a flock of starlings in the early evening sky. Nobody could make people cry the way Uncle Haafiz could.

Looking around, I saw that nobody was crying. Instead they looked as though they were feeling the exact opposite—an intense calm, even joy. Some were smiling; others had their eyes closed, looking peaceful and relaxed. Some, like the man next to me, raised their hands, while others clapped and danced a little. And all the time the small children continued to clamber over and under the chairs, picking their way through the Bibles strewn on the floor under the seats. How could anyone consider this a religion worth dying for?

When the song finished, I sat down with the others, feeling more than a little confused. The Bible study at Aunt Gulshan's was dull and lifeless, full of people who were not passionate enough to defend their ideas or give a good account of themselves. This, on the other hand, was a little different.

The rest of the service carried on in much the same way. Different people approached the front and gave messages or led prayers. A *zakir* stood up to preach, but instead of tears and silence, he brought out laughter and murmurs of agreement from the church. I did not listen much to what he said as I was too busy looking up and down my row of chairs at the people who were clearly enjoying themselves.

We sang some more, and all the time I looked about me, wondering what it was that was so different about the place. It wasn't the way the building looked or even the way the people behaved that was troubling me. There was something else. Something about the church was beyond me, and I couldn't work out what it was.

It was only when the meeting finished that I finally saw clearly for the first time. The man who had sat down beside me held out his hand. "I'm Stuart," he said.

"Ali," I replied, trying to match his smile.

"Are you a friend of Gulshan's?"

I told him she was my aunt and that I was visiting for a while from Pakistan. "I'm fifteen," I added, though I didn't know why. Perhaps I wanted him to know that I was privileged to be on an adventure so far away from home so young.

"When do you go home?"

"Two weeks," I said.

A silence fell between us, but Stuart continued to smile. I thought back to the way Stuart had been throughout the service—hands raised during the singing, laughing easily throughout the rest of the meeting—and I felt compelled to ask him more. Worrying that Aunt Gulshan might be offended by my question, I lowered my voice. "Why are you so happy?"

His smile got bigger. "I've got nothing to worry about."

"Nothing? Are you sure?"

"Yes, I'm sure. If I die I go to heaven, and if I live I get to learn more about what it means to try to follow Jesus here on earth."

I didn't know what to say. I had never met anyone quite this certain about their faith before, unless you count the Wahhabi. But this man was no Wahhabi.

"How do you know you're going to heaven?"

"I know because of Jesus. I know that he changed everything for me. All the things I did wrong but couldn't put right, he forgave me for. All the things that I thought mattered in life, he showed me what they were really worth. And I can pray to him about anything and he listens and answers. I'm never alone and I never will be, even when I die. I just know."

I did not know how to digest this, let alone how to respond. Stuart broke the silence. "What about you? How do you know you're going to heaven?"

An emptiness suddenly lurched within me. It was as if I hadn't eaten for a week. I thought about his question harder than I had ever thought about anything. How did I know? The truth was that I didn't know. I knew that many would not get in, and I was too young yet to have done any of the things I hoped to do in order to secure my place. "It is for Allah to decide." My words seemed too small for the room and they vanished like smoke.

That feeling of somehow being hollow inside stayed with me. As I followed Emily and Aunt Gulshan toward the exit, I saw a group of teenagers spilling rowdily out of a side room, laughing and joking, and I could not stop staring at them. I had always believed that Western teenagers were selfish, godless individuals with no respect for authority. I thought they were like badly behaved dogs, roaming in packs and causing trouble. I had seen enough people my age around Oxford to know that wasn't true, but seeing these teenagers at church was different. Was it possible that they could be attracted enough to Christianity to choose it instead of shopping or playing sports in the park?

That wasn't what bothered me the most, though. What struck me—although it was a gradual kind of striking, like the rise of the sun on a clear day—was the fact that I had witnessed something in church that I had never experienced in a mosque: the absence of fear.

So many times I had been in a mosque and seen people reprimanded by the *mullahs* for not being dressed appropriately, not wearing neat enough clothes, not saying the prayers in the right way, or not washing their hands correctly before coming into the prayer hall. I had even been reprimanded one day when I was seven and I'd been playing a game to see how slowly I could go from standing to sitting as the crowd bobbed up and down. I knew I was lucky not to get beaten for my foolishness, and I never misbehaved in a mosque again. But here, children were welcome to run and play.

I thought back to what it was like to visit a mosque, and remembered that I was even scared that my shoes would be stolen when I left them out in front. So I always made sure I hid them under a plant somewhere.

I found it easy enough to admit to myself that I had been scared of the *mullahs* and the petty thieves who waited like crows outside. But was I also scared of Allah? Was I fearful that I would displease him? I had never thought about it that way before, but though it pained me to admit it, I liked the atmosphere in the church. I liked the way that people were obviously relaxed during the church service. It was different. And I liked Stuart's passion. But surely feeling relaxed and being sure of your place in heaven were not enough to make someone like Aunt Gulshan turn her back on her whole family?

I knew there was more to it than that, and I knew the answer had something to do with the experience she had in her room the night she was healed. The way that she wrote about Jesus in her book reminded me of Stuart's explanation. The more I thought about it, the more I knew: the prophet Jesus was the key to all this. If I could work out what power he had over her, then I could help her to see the truth.

"I am going to a church meeting in Birmingham tomorrow," said Aunt Gulshan a few days after we had been to church. "There will be a lot of people there. You would be welcome to come."

"Is it like a *majlis*?"

"Sort of."

It was nothing like a *majlis*. There were no police blocking off the street and no crowd of *zakir* sitting on wooden thrones at the front on the stage. There were no tears from the people gathered and no haunting songs that stirred people's anger or shame.

Instead there was a small black man in a dark suit, standing at the front of a crowd of a thousand or so people wedged into a low-ceilinged building that looked more like a warehouse than a church. I felt strangely tired from the hour-long drive up from Oxford, and so I spent most of the service feeling light-headed and finding it hard to concentrate. There was the same happiness on display in many of the people around me, and the same enthusiastic singing, clapping, and dancing when a band started to play. I let it all drift over me, not really getting offended or angry about it, but just feeling quiet and kind of relaxed.

That all changed when the man in the suit said five simple words that pierced me like a spear.

"Who wants to see Jesus?"

Every single part of me heard those words. Every cell within me woke up that moment, and I felt within my chest a sudden, intense pressure that would not have been any stronger had he marched off the stage and down the aisle and shouted the words in my face while prodding me with his fist. He was speaking to me, and there was no way I could deny it.

I knew the answer was yes. I wanted to see Jesus. He was the riddle at the center of all of this, the reason Aunt Gulshan had turned her back on her family, her heritage, and her religion. He was the one who was to blame, and here was a man offering me the chance to see him for myself. If I could see him, I could put everything back the right way again.

I waited. The pressure in my chest grew stronger.

I felt sure I was about to discover what it was that had tricked Aunt Gulshan. I was about to go into the maze. So when the man spoke again, telling people to get up out of their seats and walk to the front, I didn't hesitate. I pushed back my seat and walked down with all the purpose and impatience I had ever felt.

If I had thought about it a little more, if I had given myself time to sit a while longer and think things through, I would not have gone. Like all Muslims, I believed in the prophets and I believed it was possible to see them with human eyes. But in that moment I forgot one essential teaching that had been repeated to me again and again by many different *mullahs* over the years: the prophets are only ever revealed to us in the moments before our death.

But my head was full of nothing but urgent curiosity. I was one of only a handful of people who stood at the front. I looked around me, half wondering where I should direct my gaze so as to be able to get a better view of this prophet.

The man who had invited me up came and stood in front of me. He was not quite so small now that I was near him, and his face was younger than I had first thought. "Would you like me to pray for you?" he asked.

I nodded. My voice had left me.

"Close your eyes then, son."

His hand was so hot and so heavy that the moment he placed it on my head, my eyes snapped open again. I half expected to see a giant bathed in fire in front of me, but it was just the same man, still smiling and telling me that it was okay and I could keep my eyes open if I wanted.

I closed them again. The heaviness and heat from his hand grew stronger, and for a moment my mind was flooded with the memories of Aunt Gulshan praying for me while my leg was in pain and Ami worried about the *jinn*.

The heat flowing from the man's hand grew hotter and hotter, and I had to look again to check that it was still just him who was praying for me. With my eyes open, the room seemed dark, but as soon as I closed them again, everything seemed brighter, as if someone was shining a torch onto the backs of my eyelids from within my head. The light grew brighter and brighter, and as it did, the sounds of the room—the man praying for me and the noise of others praying nearby—began to fade.

I felt my legs crumple underneath me, instantly drained of all power and strength. I fell backward, but I don't remember panicking. Instead I felt captivated by the light that was filling not just my eyes, but every part of me. I felt strong hands reach out and hold my back and shoulders, breaking my fall and guiding me gently to the floor, and heard the man who had been praying for me say, "Thank you, thank you."

His voice was quiet and distant, so small compared to the blazing light. I breathed deeply, calmly.

Though I knew that I had never had an experience quite like this, I also knew that I was safe.

That feeling changed when I heard the voice. "My son," the voice said. "You wanted to see me. I'm here. Obey me. I will forgive your sins and give you eternal life."

I knew I wasn't hearing it with my ears, that it hadn't been spoken by any man or woman around me. I knew that somehow the voice was echoing deep within me, that someone was speaking to me right there in that moment. I had nothing to compare it to, but it felt as real as the shoes on my feet and the carpet under my hands. The lights were still there and I was aware that the noises of people praying continued around me, but this voice remained within me. I felt my insides start to whirl, as if I were one of the kites I used to buy for one rupee when we were living with my grandmother.

For the first time since I left my seat and walked up to the front, I began to feel scared. Was I about to die? Was this what happened before the prophets were revealed to you? The heat I'd been feeling since the man first prayed for me was now joined by a cold sensation on my face. I was crying. Great tears as heavy as a monsoon rain were pooling in my eyes and spilling down. My breath felt heavy and trapped within me, and the tears were the only way to release it.

There was something else though, a stronger current than the fear flowing through me. I felt as though whatever was happening was something I didn't have to fight. I was at peace. If this really was death, then perhaps it wasn't so bad after all.

I don't know how long I lay there. But sometime after the light and the heat both began to fade and the tears subsided, I felt a hand on my shoulder and I opened my eyes. It was Emily. She was squatting on the floor next to me, smiling.

"Are you okay?" she asked.

I nodded and took the tissue she offered and wiped my face. "Yes," I said. My voice sounded so small. The voice of a child.

Emily guided me back to my chair. Aunt Gulshan was nearby, her hand on the shoulder of a young woman who was bent over, sobbing. Strangely, I found nothing about the scene to be troubling or unusual. It was as if I had spent all my life in places like this, weeping on the floor with *kafir*.

The car was silent on the drive home, or at least, if anyone was talking,

I did not hear them. All I could think about was the heat. The light. The voice. Yet now that those sensations had faded, the sense of peace I had felt also began to fade away. I was left only with churning questions.

The fear that had been present while I lay on the ground had increased a little as we left, and the sense of everything being all right had started to fade. I felt raw inside, empty but not hungry for food. I thought about what Ami and Baba-jan would say if I told them about this. I wondered if I could even explain to myself what had happened. How would it be possible for something to make you feel peaceful and fearful at the same time?

I was quiet as I entered the house. Zainab was asleep on the sofa downstairs, and I helped Emily guide Aunt Gulshan up to her bedroom. Both of them kept looking at me and smiling gently, and I knew they wanted me to talk about what had happened, but I could not. All I wanted was to go to my room and lie down.

Sleep came quickly. I saw colors and lights swirling in front of me as my dreams began to form. Suddenly the haze cleared and I found myself in the middle of the most vivid dream I had ever experienced. There was a strong light, just like the one I had encountered earlier that evening when my legs had crumpled and I'd fallen backward. This time I knew I was dreaming, but it didn't make the experience any less real. In fact, even if I could have opened my eyes to check that I hadn't left a light on, I wouldn't have needed to. I didn't want to leave it and I knew that this dream, with its light that seemed to hold me within it, was unlike any other.

I don't know how long I waited, resting in the light like it was a bath, but at one point I knew that something had changed. Instantly I was aware that someone else was there with me. I knew who it was. It was Jesus. I didn't know how I knew, but in this dream I couldn't find an ounce of doubt that it was him.

Where Jesus ended and the light began I could not tell. It was as if he was the light, and the light was him, but he was separate from it, a real person, physically present in my dream. I find it confusing even now, but that night in that moment, everything made sense.

And then Jesus spoke.

"Do not be afraid. I will protect you."

Unlike the time earlier in the evening when I had sensed and felt the words rather than heard them, these eight words that Jesus spoke rang louder than any noise I had ever heard in my dreams. It was as if someone were shouting them in me, but the voice was not forced or strained, not angry or wild. Instead the voice was heavy. It was like gravity. It was like the mountains. It was like truth. "Do not be afraid. I will protect you."

With that, the dream snapped shut and I jolted awake. The room was dark. I was terrified.

For a moment I could do nothing but breathe, hauling great clouds of air into my lungs. I lay there, unable even to reach out and turn on the light, just breathing. Breathing. Breathing. I looked at the clock in the hope that it would tell me the sun would soon be up and the night over. It was 3:03 a.m.

As fast as the dream had ended, my fears arrived. Everything I had learned from my religion told me that I was about to die. No man could survive what I had just experienced, much less a boy like me. And yet within me there was an opposite instinct, one that told me I didn't need to hide from this.

Not knowing which of these two opposite forces to trust, I eased my way out of bed and knocked quietly on Aunt Gulshan's door. There was no reply, but I couldn't wait until morning.

She woke quickly when I touched her shoulder.

"What is it?" She turned on the light by her bed.

"I had a dream. It was Jesus." The next words I wanted to say lay fat and heavy in my mouth, as if my jaw was not strong enough to form them. Eventually they came. "He told me not to be afraid, but I do not want to die yet."

A broad smile inched its way across her face. I had never seen her look so happy. "Ali," she said. "This is not something you need to fear. This is what happened to me."

I was shocked. In all the events of the previous evening and throughout my dream I had not connected any of this with what I had read about in Aunt Gulshan's book. Was I about to become *kafir* too?

The thought vanished from my mind as Aunt Gulshan reached out for my hand. I felt her warmth and took comfort from it.

"Jesus is inviting you to follow him, Ali. It is a wonderful thing to say yes to."

Her words had a calming effect on me, and the panic gave way to something more like peace.

"You mean I am not going to die?"

She smiled. "No."

"Why would this happen?"

"Sometimes it is because we have asked God to show himself, but sometimes it is just because God is God and he can show himself to whoever he wants. Either way, we should pray together."

Right there, in the bedroom cluttered with my aunt's prescription bottles and walker, in the soft light, I learned my first-ever prayer in Urdu—the common language of my homeland. It started by calling God a name that I had never heard used for him before, and it ended by praising him as the one with "the kingdom, the power, and the glory, forever and ever." Even though I didn't fully understand the weight of the words that formed on my lips, even though I had no idea how different my life was about to become, I knew I had found something deeply true. Something good.

I called him Father.

CHAPTER 9

A NEW KIND OF PEACE

I could still taste the tears on my tongue, still feel the weight of held breath in my lungs. I could still picture the light and hear the voice that had echoed throughout me so profoundly. Even though I had no more dreams of prophets and heard no more voices during those last two weeks in England, I awoke every morning feeling as if it were the morning after.

That night had changed everything. Here in England, I felt geographically, mentally, emotionally worlds away from Pakistan. So it was strange to think about returning home.

I was excited to see Ami and the others, of course, but unsure how recent events would change things for me once I arrived home. I had never seen that kind of light before. I had never heard that kind of voice. I had never called God "Father." It was tremendous, and beautiful, and disorienting. After such an experience, I didn't quite know what to expect or what life would look like from now on.

While I was packing my clothes into my suitcase one evening, humming an old favorite song that Ami used to sing to me when I was young, Aunt Gulshan appeared at my door and said she wanted to talk to me. Her tone and her words went against my mood, and my happy song vanished. "You need to listen to me, Ali." Her eyes were serious, sad even, and I wondered what she was going to say. "You need to know that it could be dangerous for you when you return."

I wanted to ask her to tell me more about the danger she was talking about, but I felt nervous to think how she might answer. Instead I just nodded and said that I would be careful. I knew what she meant. I was just afraid to think too closely, too carefully, about it.

"Do not be too open about your experience here," she added. "Do not talk about it with people unless you are sure that they follow Christ with all their heart as well."

As well? The phrase seemed odd to me. Was I following Jesus? I wasn't sure. Still, I was too impatient to return to my packing to question her, so I merely nodded again. She wasn't finished yet, though. "Do you remember the prayer that I taught you? The Lord's Prayer?"

"Yes." It had only taken me a day or so to commit it to memory, and I had been repeating it ever since. I liked the way it sounded. I liked the way it felt—calming and peaceful.

"Good. You must say it often."

I wondered if we were finished and started folding one of my shirts, but she had one more thing to say.

"Ali, you have met Jesus, but getting to know him has only just begun for you. There is a Bible written in English in your house. I hid it there once. Go find it and get to know it. That's one way he will continue speaking to you, though you may hear him a little differently than before."

"It is in the *bhetak*?"

Aunt Gulshan looked both surprised and pleased. "Yes, I left it there."

"I know it," I said. What I didn't tell her was that I had found it years before when Sharib and I had been terrorizing his driver by emptying all the cupboards onto the floor. Sharib had picked up the book and asked me what it was. We both looked at its thick spine and thin pages and guessed it was just some English paperback. We knew so little about Christianity that we didn't even know that's what it was.

We had used it as a substitute football one afternoon. By the time we finished, there was nothing left of it.

I decided not to tell Aunt Gulshan what Sharib and I had done to the Bible, for fear of upsetting her. Instead I determined I would find my own Bible soon after I got home. After all, my desire to learn more about Jesus would be dangerous in Lahore. I could hardly just start going to church on Sundays, not that I knew of any churches in Lahore, anyway.

The next morning, my last in England, Aunt Gulshan knocked softly on my door. "Ali, are you still angry with me like you were?"

I felt awkward, embarrassed by my behavior, which I now saw in a different light. "You mean for turning your back on Islam?" She nodded. "No," I said. "I don't think I am."

She smiled and left me alone. It was strange—I could still remember what it felt like to be angry with her, but I no longer felt the emotion myself. What did I feel instead? Confused.

On the one hand I was feeling alive and excited, as if for the first time I was seeing the world in color. My dream, the vision, and the new prayer I repeated and savored were stirring up a new appetite within me. But I also knew it came at a cost. These were dangerous dreams, subversive prayers. If I continued to embrace them, would I too end up like Aunt Gulshan, turning my back on my family?

The thought troubled me. It was far easier to think about the comforts of home, so I consciously pushed the looming questions away.

I had never been separated from Ami for as long as I had been on that trip to England, and I was missing her. I was anxious to get back, and so when the knot in my stomach grew tight from thinking about how Ami and Baba-jan would feel if they knew what had happened to me in England, I let myself daydream about the moment of my return.

I imagined them meeting me at the airport, perhaps with a garland of flowers to celebrate my and Zainab's safe return home. The very thought warmed me.

By the time my sister and I finally said goodbye to Aunt Gulshan and Emily, I was impatient about my return home. It took Zainab's tugging at my sleeve as we were swept up by the escalator to remind me to look back down at Aunt Gulshan as she waved from her wheelchair, with Emily standing behind.

It wasn't until I found my seat next to Zainab and waited for the plane to fill up that I saw more clearly what was going on. As I made my movie selections from the in-flight magazine, I noticed that my sister was crying.

"What is it?"

"We might never see Aunty again."

Her words picked a lock deep within me that I had not been aware of. Sadness broke something sharp inside. I fell silent. In all the excitement of coming home, and all the confusion and intrigue of my dream and vision, I hadn't allowed myself to think about the truth that Zainab had just expressed. But there was no doubt that Aunt Gulshan's health was frail and she was only alive because of her hospital visits. Zainab and I both knew that the chances of her being able to return to Pakistan were minimal.

Would Zainab or I ever return to England? It was unlikely. Ours had been a once-in-a-lifetime trip, the kind that none of our friends had ever taken. The chance of a return trip was even more remote than a visit from Aunt Gulshan.

I had always known that I loved Aunt Gulshan, but the six weeks we had spent living in her house had only made my feelings stronger. As a child I had seen her as mysterious and powerful, but now I understood the depth of courage it took to relocate to a foreign country alone. She had never taken a husband and she refused to allow poor health to crush her. Other women her age back in Pakistan would have retreated to the safety of their family. Yet Aunt Gulshan, with the help of Emily, was able to survive on her own.

I knew why. Having glimpsed the part of her life that she had kept hidden from the family, I knew where some of that courage came from.

Even though I knew that what I had experienced at church and alone in my room was dangerous, I didn't feel scared as I returned home. Somehow I knew that the words I had heard in my dream had some of that same power that made Aunt Gulshan so unique. He said he would protect me—and I believed him.

Yet within me were far more questions than answers. Was I a *kafir* now? I doubted it, but could I be sure? Was I going to die having seen the prophet Jesus? I didn't think so, but fifteen years of religious teaching did not evaporate overnight. Was I still a good Shia? I searched and struggled for the words to categorize my experiences, but I didn't yet know how to express what had happened to me. I didn't yet know what I now believed.

Even though my prayer mat had remained largely unused in my bag, I had prayed throughout my final two weeks in England. For the first time in my life, I was hungry for prayer. To connect with the holy. How could that be a bad thing?

Even so, I was determined to keep my experiences a secret.

As was the Islamic custom, Zainab had been allowed less freedom than me because she was a woman. She hadn't questioned what had happened when I joined the Bible study, where I had gone that Sunday morning or on the evening I accompanied Aunt Gulshan and Emily to Birmingham. If she was curious, she didn't show it, and being the firstborn male of the family, I was under no pressure to reveal any of my inner thoughts to my sister, or any of my siblings.

It turned out that keeping quiet about my experiences was not at all difficult. There was such joy and noise and bustle as we arrived back at Lahore airport that Zainab and I were immediately swept up by the crowd of family members who had gathered to witness our return.

Instead of going back home right away, we were going to spend a couple of days with Ami's cousin. I liked the plan, as Ami's cousin had a daughter called Battoul who was just two years younger than me. Battoul had eyes as dark as onyx and skin that was pale like the dawn.

I had decided long ago that she was the one I would marry, and I was excited for any opportunity to spend time in her company.

Like every other boy my age, my choice of a marriage partner was not a private one. Instead it was a matter of family concern. Many in the West think of these marriages as forced, though the tradition is more true to its name—arranged marriages. It becomes a family discussion and arrangement. When I was fourteen Ami had already told me that she and Baba-jan were thinking that I would marry a certain cousin, though not Battoul. I had objected and she had relented and I knew then that if I was to marry Battoul, I would first need to secure Ami and Baba-jan's consent.

Unfortunately, I forgot all that as we relaxed in their house a few hours after landing. I was sipping sweet chai and eating sweets and telling the gathered relatives all about life in England, especially about the size of the supermarkets and the number of different ethnicities— how the whole world could be seen on just one street. Battoul's little brothers were running around, pulling at my hand to get me to show them some more of the English coins that I had brought back with me. I was feeling good, and Battoul, her parents and grandparents, plus Ami were all listening carefully to what I had to say. Emboldened, I decided to swallow down my nerves and introduce the subject of my future.

"Now that I have been to England," I said, clearing my throat, "I am ready to become a man." There were smiles and one or two nods from the adults. My throat closed a little, but a sip of chai loosened it up again. "I will finish my studies, then start a business." More nods this time. One more quick sip of chai for me, and then I jumped off the cliff. "And I would like to marry Battoul."

To my surprise, when I looked up from my cup, the smiles had vanished from the adults' faces. I checked for Battoul's reaction, but she had slipped out of the room.

"Well," said Ami, with a glint of warning in her eyes, "we shall discuss this later, Ali." Her using my name like that was not a good sign, and when the room cleared soon after, she let me know how unhappy she was with me.

"It was not your place to say that," she said, spitting out the words like they were soured milk. "That was *not* the right way to go about it."

She walked briskly away, but I could tell the discussion was not over. We stayed at Battoul's house for the night, and though I wanted to talk to her the next day at breakfast, she was too busy helping her grandmother for me to have the opportunity.

By the time we arrived back home later that day, Ami had forgiven me for embarrassing her and I was able to discuss some of my other plans for the future. I told her I didn't see any point in carrying on my education after high school and so would not be going to university. I also told her I was a man now, and as such, I needed a motorbike.

"Well," she said, "I agree."

"You do?"

"About the motorbike. But nothing else. You are the firstborn son and Baba-jan is a lawyer who will one day become a politician. Of course you will go to university, Nomi."

It was typical of Ami, making me feel grown up and important while at the same time gently reminding me of who was really in charge. I decided to be pleased about the news of the motorbike and put from my mind the thought of having to continue my education by attending university.

"It is good to be home," I said, smiling back at Ami.

My first few days back were even more of a wild time than our arrival back at the airport. Friends came to visit me at home, and others I knew less well crowded around me at Uncle Faizal's, eager for news of what life was really like in England.

"How was your trip?"

"Can you help me to go to England too?"

"Is it true that you flew first class?"

Apparently rumors had been flying.

It was good to be home, and even starting back at school the next week wasn't quite the torture it usually was. In corridors and lunch queues I still had plenty of boys approach me and ask about England. After a month, just when the interest was dying down, my popularity received another significant boost. I came downstairs one morning to see Baba-jan holding out a shiny silver key on a black leather keychain.

"Nomi," he said, "you should take this with you and go look outside."

I was too excited to say anything but did exactly as he said, followed by everybody else in the house. There in the courtyard, next to his Range Rover and Ami's Honda, was a sleek-looking motorbike, just like Sharib's, with a red tank and chrome guards. I looked back at Ami to check, and she just smiled and gestured for me to climb on and start it up.

The questions that I had buried deep inside me—*Who, what, do I believe? Am I kafir now?*—still returned from time to time and kept me awake at night. But on a surface level, life was good.

Every day I drove around on my 125cc bike, picking up two or three friends on the way to school, drifting my way through lessons before returning home for a shower and an evening out on the bike with yet more friends.

The streets were only ever quiet late at night, and I quickly got the hang of weaving in and out of the odd mixture of traffic. Between the rickshaws and donkeys, horses pulling carts and people pushing trolleys and bicycles along, there were more than enough opportunities for me to practice emergency stops and quick escapes. I even managed to perfect my wheelies, but gave that up after trying it with Misim clinging to my back and getting caught by Baba-jan.

"I saw you doing those stunts earlier," he raged at me when I got home that night. "What were you thinking of? If you both get killed, I'll have no sons at all."

His words were powerful. To leave a man without sons would be like leaving him and Ami without a home. It would leave them to face old age without financial security, protection, or any hope at all. Everything that he had built with his career—all his social status and wealth—would vanish. It was the same reason my father hadn't bothered to try to kidnap Zainab but instead had focused solely on me, his son.

I told him I was sorry and promised not to do it again. I hated the idea of leaving Ami and Baba-jan in a terrible position like that, but having been to England, I wondered whether someone my age there would feel the same. Would the boys who had been rude to me on the basketball court bow to their parents' will so easily? I had grown up knowing that Western children were disrespectful of their elders and roamed independently, but having been there myself, I noticed there was a part of me that envied their ability to be rude and disrespectful.

As the months passed, what really settled in my mind were not these thoughts about the differences between East and West, but the difference within myself since I returned. I felt unsettled and awkward whenever Friday came around and the men in the house prepared to go to the mosque for prayers. I found myself making excuses to Ami in order to avoid going altogether. For Baba-jan, this was never a problem. He believed that one of the privileges of being a Sayed was that we didn't have to go to the mosque as often as other men of lower birth. But Ami was less sure and took more convincing from me before she would allow me to just pray at home.

"I just want to be a humble Muslim," I told her one day when she asked again why another Friday had passed and I stayed home during prayers. "I don't want to be like those men who want to go to the mosque to show people how important and how holy they are. I just want to do what's right, be a good person who serves Allah without any of the show."

"You're right," she said. "And we have noticed a difference in you since you returned. You seem . . ."

For some reason I felt unexpectedly nervous when she said this, and the pause while she looked for the words to finish her sentence was painful and set my heart racing. "I don't know what the difference is, I can't say, but whatever it is we like it. You can stop going to the mosque, but just make sure you keep on praying at home."

Those nerves surprised me and left me feeling confused. What had I been worried about? I didn't know, but I remembered Aunt Gulshan's advice to be careful. Was this the kind of danger I needed to avoid? This was Ami, after all.

In the same way that I avoided the mosque, I started to go off prayer the way a sick person goes off food. Whenever I unrolled my mat and began the ritual of washing myself in preparation for prayer, I felt awkward and conflicted. So I gave up. For weeks I isolated myself from Allah, acting as if there was an invisible, impenetrable barrier between us.

It didn't work.

Instead of feeling free and in control of my own life, I simply felt lost and alone. It was as if someone had brought a thick fog into my world and stolen from the sun all its heat and light. All was gray in those days, and I didn't like it at all. Worse than the feeling itself was the fact that none of it made any sense at all. Since I'd returned from England, I'd declared who I wanted to marry, had the shiny new keys to a motorbike, was getting on well enough at school, and was being allowed the kind of freedom to choose not to go to the mosque. I was becoming a man, so why was I feeling like this?

Deep down, I knew why. I had met Jesus, and life could never go back to the way it was. I thought back to that strange night that I feared might be my last, lying on the church floor, drinking in all that glorious light.

I wanted more. I wanted to talk to a Christian, to find a Bible to make up for the one Sharib and I had destroyed all those years before. I wanted answers—or at least someone to explain if what was happening to me was typical of all people who went to church.

Finding a Christian in Pakistan was not easy, particularly for a

Sayed. Christianity was the religion of the street sweepers, a collection of outcasts and misfits, of those who failed to belong elsewhere. The chances of my knowing one of these people well enough to talk to them openly about such a delicate matter was slim, and the chance of one of them being willing to talk to a Sayed in return, and risk being accused of trying to convert a good Muslim boy away from Islam, was nonexistent. No *umti* would risk his life like that.

Fortunately, I went to a Catholic school. Even though I had never heard any of them talk about it, I knew some of my teachers were Christians. There was good reason for their silence; attempting to convert a Muslim away from the faith is punishable by death in Pakistan. And besides, our community considered Christians to be from the lowest castes. They were almost invisible.

But it didn't matter. They had something I needed. So one week before my sixteenth birthday, instead of climbing on my motorbike and speeding home at the end of school, I made my way down dusty corridors in search of the one teacher who I thought might be willing to talk.

I found him alone in a room, quietly putting back chairs and desks that had been disturbed in the typical rush for the door. He wasn't many years older than me and only a little taller. He seemed like someone I could trust.

He looked up as I came in. *"Al-salamu alaykum,"* I said, greeting him as I did every other person I met.

"Wa alaykum," he replied.

I hadn't planned what I was going to say, so I just launched into it. "I want to know what it means to be a Christian."

He looked as though I had just pulled out a gun. "Don't talk to me about it," he said, looking over my shoulder to make sure nobody outside might have overheard me talk. "You must not joke about that kind of thing."

"I'm not joking. I'm serious. Can you get me a Bible?"

Eyes wide, hands up in defense, he was panicked. It was no use.

Before I could say anything else, he had made his way to the door and was ushering me out. "Please," he said. "Do not ask me this anymore."

I left and made my way home. I was frustrated by his reluctance to talk, and when the electricity went out at the house, causing the ceiling fans to come to a halt and the air inside the house to grow stale and lifeless, I made my way up to the roof in hope of a breeze and some relief from the nagging dissatisfaction that had been present in me for weeks.

I found none. I just felt annoyed. I was frustrated by the teacher's fear and I was frustrated by my own lack of peace. I should have been happy and optimistic, with everything lined up ahead of me, and yet nothing was making sense. The power cut was just another reminder of the way that things were not working as they should have.

I thought back to my time in England. That was where it had all started to go wrong for me. Since then I had been unable to pray. Every time I tried, my tongue stuck in my throat. It was as if I had forgotten how to speak the words that usually flowed so freely from me. To whom was I supposed to be praying? Allah or the Christ, this Jesus man who had appeared to me so powerfully?

The sun was hot on the roof and there was no breeze to speak of, but I was too cross to move again now, so I fell on some cushions laid out in a shaded corner. I closed my eyes and thought back to the last few days in England. I remembered how warm Aunt Gulshan's hand felt on mine the night I woke her up to tell her about my dream. I remembered the way she was so keen to remind me to be careful about my return. And I remembered the words Jesus said to me as I lay rigid in my bed. He told me not to be afraid. "I will protect you," I said under my breath. "I will protect you."

Feeling the heat of the evening sun as it bit its way through the shade of the tarpaulin stretched across the roof, I remembered the way the light had felt in my dream, as well as in the vision I had earlier at the church as I lay on the floor. The light had been so bright both times that I had felt it with my whole body, but there was something else about it too, a sense that somehow the light itself was good, that I had no reason to fear it.

My memory was only a pale reflection of that light, but even just that memory was enough to comfort me. My frustration began to melt away, and I found myself recalling the power of the voice that had thundered through my dream. In just the same way that the light was more than bright, so the voice was more than loud. It was truth, it was power, it was everything. I hadn't known just how hungry I was for it until I experienced it for myself.

I don't know how long I stayed up on the roof, but by the time I sat up and made my way down, it was getting dark. The air was cooler, smooth against my skin. But it was inside that I felt the change. I couldn't remember the last time I'd felt this kind of peace.

CHAPTER 10

IS THIS HOW I DIE?

"Jesus, if it's really you, would you help me?"

It felt a little odd to be talking out loud like this, my words half-whispered in case anyone overheard, but it also felt strangely right.

The roof quickly became my sanctuary. I began talking to Jesus as if he were right there, standing on the top of the house with me. I was spending more and more time on my own up there, retreating from the confusion that always seemed to accompany any Islamic customs—visits from the *mureed*, prayer at the mosque, ceremonial fasting.

I used to spend my days on the rooftop flying kites, chasing that sensation of flying. But now I spent them searching for peace. And there among the cushions and shade, the vines that grew overhead, and the unrivaled views over the crowded streets that spread out before me like a spider's web, I found it.

I developed a routine, which always started with my lying down and recalling in as much detail as possible the events of that night back in England. And when I reached the part where Jesus appeared in my dream and spoke to me, I tried extra hard to savor every moment of the experience. I let the words he spoke flood right through me, recalled the way the light felt upon me, and heard his voice call to the deepest parts of me.

Having bathed in these memories again, I would then pray. I prayed for Aunt Gulshan's health, for my studies, my future, and the well-being of my family. If any of my *mureed* had asked me to pray for them in the days before, I would pray for them as well. And this time I wouldn't forget, because now I was praying to Jesus. Though I knew nothing more about him than what he had told me in my dream, something within me knew he was the only one to whom I should be praying.

These moments became precious to me. I would end them by standing and staring out across the rooftops. I'd see kites racing through the sky and listen to the shouts of children both celebrating and despairing at the battles taking place in the clouds above them. I remembered the days when as a child I would have joined them, though I knew all that was behind me now.

I never knew how desperate I had been for peace until I found it in these moments. But when I came back down, I found the contrast between this newfound calm and the Muslim faith increasingly wide.

Throughout my childhood in Pakistan, my favorite time of year was always Eid. After the hard month of Ramadan, where like everyone I fasted during the day and ate only at night, I always appreciated the chance to celebrate. Eid was like Christmas and Easter rolled into one, a unique time of feasting and generosity, of charity and unity.

My first Eid after I arrived back from England took place shortly after I got my motorbike. Even though I was having fun and enjoying my newfound freedom, I started to see the celebrations through different eyes. Ramadan had started soon after I arrived back in the country, and by the time the month had finished, I felt as though I had lost my appetite for Allah, even though this season was designed to strengthen it. If I tried to read the Qur'an, I felt suddenly tired, and whenever I tried to pray, I fell mute. The food that usually occupied my dreams for many of the nights leading up to the feast tasted like paper on my tongue, and the crowds that made their way to the mosque, while usually so full of people I knew and cared for, seemed to me to be full of faceless strangers.

It wasn't just big public events. I also stopped wanting to join Ami,

Baba-jan, and the other children on our family's weekly visits to the country club. It was a fine place, and before England, I had always enjoyed the time we spent there. It was full of politicians, judges, and lawyers like Baba-jan, and it offered everything from horse riding to computer games and a swimming pool. It was a place for the elite of society, and there was a time when I loved to indulge the sense of privilege and confidence that saturated the place. But once I discovered the peace and power of my times on the roof, the country club held no attraction for me. I no longer cared that people were impressed by the fact that I was a member there. As a currency it lost all its value in one giant crash. Whenever Ami told me they were going, I would make up some excuse and stay behind, relishing the knowledge that I could pray undisturbed for hours while they were out.

The only sport that I missed from the club was badminton, but I discovered that playing on the patch of wasteland out behind our house with a handful of poor kids was even more fun than playing on a purpose-built court with the son of a man who would one day likely make a run for some high political office. There was more laughter out on the wasteland, more life in the eyes of the children who had never owned shoes before.

I started giving money to kids like these, and then to other poor people as well. I took to cleaning my own shoes and being nice to the servants, and I developed a strong dislike of ever being waited on. And when a ten-year-old kid whom Ami had hired to help Zainab was no longer needed, I was in no doubt what we needed to do.

"We must pay for the girl to go to school," I said to Ami.

She looked a little surprised, but agreed quickly enough.

"Nomi," she said as I was about to leave, but when I turned back, she just smiled and told me that she had forgotten what she was going to say.

As the academic year came to a close and I started to think about the long summer vacation, I took a trip on my bike to Sharib's house.

There was a crowd outside, with more than two hundred of his family's *mureed* gathering for prayer and advice. Neither Sharib nor any of his family had come out to the courtyard yet, so I just joined the back of the line and waited my turn to talk to a servant who was quizzing people at the main door.

"Are you waiting for prayer too?" he asked me once my long wait was over.

"No. I am just a friend of Sharib."

The servant looked skeptical until Sharib's voice called out from a window on the first floor.

"Nomi! It's you!" A few seconds later he emerged from the main door holding a chair and a bottle of water. "What are you doing here like this? You know you don't have to wait outside like all the others."

"I know," I said, "but I don't mind so much." I had been happy enough sitting outside with the rest of the people. A year or so before, I would have marched up to the front and demanded to be admitted right away. But things were different now. So much of what I once loved about being a Sayed had started to cause me discomfort. It was like milk that had just started to turn sour—appearing normal to the eye, but curdling once inside you to make you want to spit it out.

That long summer drifted by slowly, and in many ways I was happy with the changes that were taking place within me. I knew I was becoming a better version of myself, but I also knew my life could not stay this way—this easy, this comfortable. I just didn't know what would happen next.

It was Ami who helped me to face up to what was growing inside me, even though she had no knowledge of what she was doing. "You have changed, Nomi," she said one afternoon as I came down from the roof. "You don't fight anymore; you don't go out so much. You help around the house and you're even looking after Misim. What is it?"

I wanted to tell her everything, to start with Aunt Gulshan's book and go on to tell her about church and the vision and the dream and how life had felt different ever since. I wanted to tell her that in some ways these changes were all deliberate, all the result of my following a new set of instincts that I had somehow acquired. I also wanted to tell her that I was terrified by it all, that I was starting to feel ordinary, as if I mattered no more or less than any other *umti* on the street, and I wished it would stop. But I couldn't say any of this. Instead I rolled out my well-worn line. "I just want to be a better Muslim. I want to be humble. I don't want to be proud."

This time Ami didn't leave it there. "Well, we do like the change that we see in you, Nomi, but you must not neglect the mosque. Take Misim with you now and go to pray. The *mullahs* will be pleased to see you after so long."

The thought of visiting the mosque made my palms sweat. My new instincts told me it wasn't a good place for me, though I wasn't completely sure why. But how could I refuse Ami?

Misim and I made the ten-minute walk last for twenty, him chattering away about school and life and his favorite cricketer. We arrived at the mosque, and that's when I saw it. A thick, rusted chain was slung across the main gate, held in place by a heavy padlock. Misim tugged at it, but the lock held fast. He turned back and shrugged.

It was odd—the mosque was always open at this time of the afternoon. I looked around, wondering if anyone else was surprised by the lock, but if they were, they didn't show it. The crowded street bustled on around us as usual. No one gave the lock a second look.

With no other option, we turned around and walked home.

Ami seemed satisfied with my explanation, especially when Misim backed me up and described the lock. I thought that was the end of the discussion. But the next day she brought up the subject again.

"I spoke to one of the *mullahs* who was at the mosque all day yesterday," she said as I was heading up to the roof. "He said the gate was not locked at all. He said that they have not locked it for weeks."

She folded her arms and looked me straight in the eye, daring me to lie to her. I felt a sudden weight of guilt, my chest began to sink within me. For what reason, though? The gate truly had been locked, unless I was going crazy. But if I was crazy, then Misim was too.

No words came to my defense. After the silence between us grew more painful by the second, Ami spread her hands and looked up at the sky. I knew I was forgiven.

When I closed my eyes at night, I dreamed of locked gates that suddenly exploded open when I reached out to touch them. Every time they opened, they revealed a hollow blackness beyond them, a darkness that terrified me.

What did it mean? Had the gate really been locked, or had I imagined it? Was I beginning to lose my mind, to hallucinate things that were not there? Had it been a test from Allah, and what would happen to me now that I had failed? Or had Jesus locked them to keep me away from the mosque? And why would he want that?

The one thing I was sure about was the fact that the padlock perfectly illustrated how I felt about Islam. I felt barred from it, removed and distant. Everything that I had been brought up to believe about it, just like everything I'd been brought up to believe about myself as a Sayed, stopped making sense. My life of privilege for which I'd so recently been greedy no longer held any appeal for me.

I was beginning to feel like an *umti*—an outsider. It terrified me. If I was not a Sayed, if I was not a Shia, then what was I?

While I was experiencing my own inner turmoil, my homeland also was going through its own religious identity crisis—often resulting in violence. Wahhabi attacked Shia with even greater force and frequency than I could ever remember, and it seemed as though every week brought a fresh batch of horrific pictures of bodies covered in dust and blood being dragged from bomb sites by men who looked as though their souls had been blasted away too. One week it was a Shia mosque and the next it was a city hotel. Sometimes a suicide bomber would strike in the middle of a civil protest, other times in a busy market. Always for the same reason—the centuries-old conflict between Wahhabi and Shia.

Even though the location changed with every news report, the men behind the violence remained the same.

"It is all the fault of the Americans." I heard this line so many times from so many different people. "As soon as they pushed the Taliban out of Afghanistan, they came here, so they are killing us now."

Throughout the year the same stories kept on coming, piling up like the bodies I saw on the news. And with every new headline, the sense that I no longer belonged to this world of religious hatred grew deeper and deeper.

I was out with Sharib one afternoon late in December, making a rare visit to Uncle Faizal's, when my phone rang. It was Ami.

"Get home now!" There was no hesitation in her voice, no patience, no preamble. It was simply an order. I didn't want to stay out long enough to discover what sort of danger she was talking about.

I pulled Sharib by the arm and we sprinted to my bike, the engine roaring as we drove off. Once inside the gate, we burst into the house to find everyone—the servants, the children, Ami and Baba-jan too—staring at the television in the lounge. The same familiar images played across the screen. Bodies and blood and dust, police and ambulances and reporters, tears and anger and shock.

"They killed Bhutto," said Baba-jan. I had never seen him look so angry. He had always talked about Benazir Bhutto as a woman of principle who had been critical of the Taliban and the terrorist acts committed by their followers. She was a sign that life in Pakistan could improve. She had served as our prime minister twice, lived in exile for years, and finally, just two months earlier, had returned to Pakistan to stand for election.

Baba-jan, his fists clenched and his jaw locked tight, stared at the screen. It was hard to say how many people had died with her, but she had been appearing at a rally and it looked as though the numbers included innocent supporters as well as security guards.

"She will have *shahid*," Baba-jan said quietly when he had finally seen enough. Like any soldier who died on the battlefield, Bhutto had died a martyr's death and would go straight to heaven. I murmured my agreement, but the words tasted all wrong in my mouth.

I left and went up to the roof to think. What if Aunt Gulshan returned to Pakistan? Would the same fate await her as well? And what about *shahid* and the idea of going to heaven; would she have *shahid* too, even if she had turned her back on Islam? And what of Jesus? He told me that he would protect me, but could he protect someone like Aunt Gulshan from a Wahhabi in a suicide vest?

I thought about the family of whatever Wahhabi had killed himself that day. They would be mourning him in his family home that night, and the sound of sobbing and wailing would echo far down the streets. They too would be claiming that he had died a martyr's death.

All my life I had loved Islam. It had taught me how to pray, how to spend my money, how to dress, how to eat, and how to live almost every aspect of my life. It had been my sun and my moon, my air and my earth. I had never questioned it any more than I had questioned gravity. It was as much a part of me as the hair on my head. And yet something about it—or about me—had changed. Though I loved Baba-jan and wanted to believe his talk of Bhutto and *shahid*, it made no sense to me. How could both killer and victim be welcomed into the same heaven?

And yet, when I thought about heaven and eternal life, I did not feel downcast. I remembered the light I had seen in the church, in my dreams. Somewhere within me were the first shoots of optimism. Somehow, I believed that the words Jesus had spoken to me were real.

The air was spiked with tension at school the next morning. The previous day's assassination was all anyone was talking about, and being a minority Shia kid in a school full of Sunni with a handful of

Wahhabi, I knew I should keep my opinions about Bhutto's innocence to myself. I managed to do just that, although I could feel the frustration increase with every conversation I overheard about Bhutto being a traitor or the judgment of Allah on those who fell foul of the law. It was typical Wahhabi propaganda, but there was no point in trying to argue against it.

I made it all the way to the end of the school day, but then I broke. I was sitting on the grass outside the main entrance, whiling away a few lazy minutes with a handful of friends. They were talking about the right way of sacrificing an animal in order to be absolved of your sins. My mind snapped back to the first vision I had when I was in England: the bright lights and the sense that I was inhaling the words of God. "My son," the voice had said. "You wanted to see me. I'm here. Obey me. I will forgive your sins and give you eternal life."

Their speculation about what type of animal worked best for each type of sin sounded foolish in comparison with the words of God, and in that moment I knew beyond all doubt that forgiveness was not found in the killing of an animal. It wasn't something that needed to be bought or bargained for. Forgiveness was something that had already been offered. All we had to do was know where to find it.

I didn't really think about what I was about to say, and in the moments before opening my mouth, I felt nothing other than a slight surge of anger and an odd lightness within me.

"You are wrong," I said. "Sacrificing an animal is not the right way to deal with sin. I had a dream when I was in England that showed me the truth. If you want to know how to deal with sin, you have to pray to Jesus."

In the silence, I felt their stares upon me.

"You're lying," said Yazie, one of the eldest among us. "How can you say that Jesus can forgive sins? What you're saying is a sin itself."

"I am not making it up, Yazie," I said. "You can pray too if you like. See for yourself."

He got up with a huff and left, and the others followed soon after.

I tried to put the incident from my mind as I returned home, and throughout the next day when I was back at school I thought how good it was that the school year would be over in a few weeks. At the end of the day I was alone in a classroom, putting away some chairs, when Yazie appeared at the door. He was a big guy, and a class clown. This time, however, he looked serious.

"Come on, Nomi," he said. "Let's go."

I thought he was simply telling me that it was time for us to leave, maybe go to Uncle Faizal's. I followed him out one of the side doors of the school and noticed two of his cousins standing nearby. As soon as they saw us they walked quickly toward me. *Perhaps we are not going to Uncle Faizal's after all*, I thought.

They started with pushes and slaps. I did my best to defend myself, and though I was smaller than them, I was fast. I was also full of frustration that had been building up for the year and a half since I returned from England. I was fed up with feeling as though things had stopped making sense.

And though I did not know why they were pushing me around, I welcomed the outlet to swing back, to tighten my fists against all the things I didn't understand.

None of us said a word—not me, not Yazie as he stood behind me and pushed me repeatedly away from the doorway that led back into the school, and not his two cousins who had progressed from slapping to punching me.

There was only silence. Silence and the sudden smack of fist against skin, scuffling in the dirt.

Yazie and his cousins probably just want to remind me of my place as a Shia in a country dominated by Sunni, I told myself. *Give it a few moments and they'll soon tire and go home.*

But then they moved in together, a circle of muscle all around me, forcing me down to the ground. I felt a sharp pain nip at my back as

I landed on a rock. I tried to will it to pass, and in the pause as they pinned me down by my arms and legs, I wondered whether I would need more than Sharib to exact my revenge on them the next day.

The silence was broken by an unfamiliar voice. I didn't understand the words at first but looked up to see that we had been joined by a man old enough to be Yazie's father or uncle. He was wearing a white *shalwar kameez* and had a full beard and a long green and yellow turban piled high on his head and trailing down over his shoulder. I had never seen him before, but I could tell from his clothing that he was a Wahhabi.

It took me a moment to realize that he was speaking Arabic. "You tried to make *kafir* out of our children. Islam gives me the right to kill any infidel who does that or who speaks against our beloved prophet."

Kafir. Infidel. The words echoed in my rising fear.

I tried to resist the urge to panic by reminding myself that Wahhabi were always talking like this, always declaring that the Qur'an gave them the right to kill this person or that person. However, when I saw him reach into his pocket and pull out a switchblade, I felt defenseless against the terror.

Again there was silence as he moved in toward me. Besides the muffled sounds of my legs and arms struggling against the hands of Yazie and his cousins, the only noise I heard was the blade springing out of the handle.

The man with the turban moved up close to me, just a foot away from my face. Yazie had my shoulders pinned and I could see him looking down at the knife, with its blade a little longer than my hand. "Hold him tighter," said the man. I looked and saw his eyes measuring up my chest and his free hand reaching out to pin me down. He held the blade steady above my heart.

My only thought in that moment was I was not ready to die. I knew I had to try to escape. I also knew it was impossible, but I threw every last bit of my strength into my shoulders, twisting and yanking in an effort to avoid the blade as he drove it into me. I felt white fire searing my chest, fierce and hot. I saw his right hand pull back, saw the blood drip from the blade and tried to shout.

The pain left me mute and robbed me of the ability to breathe. I fought to bring air into my lungs, but a fresh blast of pain scorched itself across my chest. "Again," said the man, bringing the knife back down. This time I was able to get an arm free and bring it across me, a fragile shield against the blade.

I could see nothing, just my hand, a glimpse of steel. I couldn't struggle anymore. I had no strength left. Suddenly I felt their hands on me again, and the world tipped—the buildings above me slipped from my view. They dragged me through the dust and dropped me under a bush. Then I heard footsteps trailing off into the darkness.

I tried to sit up, but the pain clouded my thoughts and movements like thick, dark smoke. I fell backward, and only then did I see my chest was covered in blood. I took one final look up at the bush above me and the sky beyond it and closed my eyes.

No time to think. Just sleep.

CHAPTER 11

MY NAME ON THEIR HIT LIST

The second time I saw Jesus was very different from the first. When it happened in England, I knew that I was asleep and that if I didn't get swept up to heaven, I would wake up and be back in the little bedroom in Aunt Gulshan's house.

On this second occasion, I didn't even know whether I was dead or alive.

It started with the light. Just as before, I was surrounded by it, swimming in its bright depth. My fear melted away in its presence. It was just me and the light. No fear, no panic, nothing other than the strange contentment and peace that came from being right where I was.

I recognized Jesus instantly. It is hard for me to describe him, for even though he was physical like any man, with a face and hands and hair and the rest, these were not the things that told me it was him. Just like the light filled me with a sense of its goodness, so every bit of me just knew that it was Jesus who was standing before me. I knew it. Every part of me knew it.

He looked at me.

Mountains could have formed and oceans could have run dry in that moment. It could have lasted a thousand years or it could have passed in the beat of a bird's wing. I had no idea where or when I was. All I knew was that he was able to see everything about me.

Still the light was there. Still the peace.

Up until this point, I had felt no pain, but I soon became aware of it again. Yet it paled in comparison with the light and the knowledge that Jesus was right there with me. I knew I had been hurt, but it didn't seem to matter all that much.

"You were injured because you were defending me," he said. "I will not let you die."

Jesus reached out his right hand and placed it on the wound on the left side of my chest.

"I will protect you."

I opened my eyes. Green walls. Peeling paint. Stale air laced with the smell of chemicals. The backs of my legs sticking to something plastic. My head tipped too far back. The sound of voices speaking too far away for me to understand. The pain in my chest that felt as though it had burrowed deeper than ever, right into my bones and out the other side.

But then there was Ami standing above me, tears streaking her cheeks. A look in her wide eyes that I struggled to read. Was it fear? Shock? Joy?

Another face appeared. A man's, someone I vaguely recognized. A doctor? Yes, that was it. He looked into my eyes and I felt his hands press me this way and that. He was looking for something, but he didn't know what. *Jesus didn't look at me that way*, I thought. When he looked, he saw everything. This man was almost overwhelmed by confusion.

Eventually I felt my body grow heavier, sinking deep into the plastic mattress I was lying on. I let myself go. The exhaustion was too much for me.

When I woke up, Ami was right there with me. She gasped, put her hand to her mouth, and leaned over to kiss me, but there was none of the shock that I had seen in her eyes before. All I saw in her was pure joy.

"Nomi!" she said. "You're alive!"

Over and over she repeated herself, holding my hand and giving way to new tears and smiles. I heard another voice, felt another hand at my side, and looked over to see Sharib. He was smiling too, but the smile didn't reach his eyes.

"The security guard found you," he said. "He brought you here." He looked over to Ami then quickly back to me. He clamped his mouth shut. I thought I saw a gun in the waistband of his trousers, but I couldn't be sure.

"The doctor said that you have lost a lot of blood," said Ami. "He said that the knife missed your heart but went through to your lung." The tears came heavier again, and she had to pause for a moment. "He said that there was nothing they could do here, that there wasn't time to get you to a hospital where they could operate. He said you were going to die."

I remembered Jesus, his hand on my chest and his words. And I knew. He was the one who had saved me. He was the one who had protected me, just like his promise from the dream. He was the one who had given me back my life.

Later, when the doctor examined me, he told me that he couldn't explain where the blood that had filled my left lung had gone. It had simply vanished. I knew I had an answer for him, but I didn't speak. I just pretended to be tired again and he soon left me alone.

It wasn't until the next day that I started to understand what had really happened and what was now at stake. Sharib came to visit, and when we were alone, he leaned over and spoke quietly.

"There are a lot of people outside. At first they were angry that someone would do this to Baba-jan's son. But then the rumors started up." He paused. When he spoke again, his voice was even quieter, almost a whisper. "Is it true what Yazie says? Did you tell him to pray to Jesus?"

I felt my throat tighten and a vicious thirst scratch its way right down to my stomach. I didn't want to answer Sharib at all, but what use was there in lying? I nodded.

He arched his eyebrows and puffed his cheeks, blowing out a long, heavy breath. "You need to go to the newspapers and tell them you were joking."

I understood why he wanted me to do this, but I knew it was impossible. In the hours that I had spent awake on that bed, something had changed within me. I'd gone from being someone who was merely interested in Jesus to being someone who owed him his life.

"No," I said. "I cannot."

His eyes flashed at me, and when he spoke, his voice was rough, angry. "At least tell your mother that it was a joke. Let her tell others. Perhaps that will be enough to calm people down for a while."

"No." I smiled. "I don't care if they are angry."

"You don't care? After I was here with you yesterday, I went to find them. I had a gun with me and was ready to kill them myself. But the police had arrested them already."

"They are in jail?" I felt encouraged by the thought of it.

"No! They only held them for an hour or two. As soon as the police found out that they attacked you for being apostate, they dropped the charges. That's when the rumors started."

The silence returned. So did my fear. Again it was Sharib who spoke first.

"What you have done will cause us all problems. Unless you take your words back, apologize, and say that you are not going to take any of them to court, you are making trouble for every one of us in your family. And none of us can protect you."

I remembered Jesus' words. They were all I could remember.

I was left alone for much of the time after that. Apart from Ami, who occasionally brought Misim and Zainab with her, I spent the next ten days lying on my own in the medical center, left alone with my thoughts. Sharib did not return, and on the two occasions when Baba-jan appeared, he only stood at the edge of the room and said nothing.

I did not mind so much. The room was quiet and I was able to think. Sharib's words refused to fade, and I thought much about the fact that my actions were causing pain for people in my family. I hated that and wished it could be different. But I knew what had happened could not be undone.

In many ways these days were just an extension of my time on the roof, only this time I had not just one vision of Jesus to reflect on, but two. I savored them both, replaying them in my mind, feeling again the echo of the light, his voice and his touch.

In time, though, I had to go home. And when I did, a storm was waiting for me.

Baba-jan picked me up from the medical center and we made the ten-minute drive back to the house in total silence. It wasn't until we arrived home and he pulled the Range Rover in through the gate that he finally spoke.

"Why didn't you tell me anything about this before?"

"About what?" I said. He glared at me, obviously considering giving me a slap. What had he wanted me to tell him about? Did he know about the dream and the visions, or was he talking about my praying to Jesus up on the roof?

"I have given you everything," he said, "so why are you doing this to me?"

He was right, of course. Baba-jan was a pillar in the community—respected, wealthy, a man of means and influence. Because of him, because he had accepted me even as a stepson, I had inherited all this and more.

I had no response that I could summon quick enough, and by the time I had climbed out of the car, he had crossed the courtyard and was inside the house. Ami came to help me and guided me inside.

Baba-jan was not finished, though. "You need to take it back and put things right," he said, shouting now. He turned to Ami, waving his hand in frustration. "Tell your son that he's going stupid." He walked back out the front door, slamming it behind him.

I hadn't seen Baba-jan like that before, and it made me nervous. Ami was anxious too, though instead of shouting, her voice was soft and soothing.

"He's right," she said. "A lot of people are talking about what happened and they are all angry with you. Just tell them that it was a joke. If you do that then Baba-jan can make things right."

Just as in the conversation with Sharib, I knew I couldn't grant her wish. This time, however, I was clearer in my mind about why. Now I knew there was a reason Jesus had told me in my dream that he would protect me. I was in danger, my life was at risk, and Jesus not only knew it but was the only one capable of keeping me safe. Without him I would be dead. He was the only one I could trust, and to turn my back on him would be suicide.

I looked at Ami and wondered if there was any way I could explain all this. "It was not a joke. It was all real. Ami, I was dead, but now I'm alive."

"Nomi—" she began, but I interrupted her.

"I'm serious. When I was lying on the bed, before I woke up after they stabbed me, I saw Jesus. He touched me here," I said, wincing a little as I lifted my left arm. "The doctor was right and you were right too; I really was going to die. But Jesus healed me. He saved my life."

I watched Ami as she took in the words. She looked confused at first, then serious. She stared at me. I tried a different approach.

"If it was a different prophet who had appeared to me, you would all be happy right now. There would be crowds of people coming to see me and the family would all be happy. But because it was Jesus who revealed himself, you're all angry. It makes no sense to me. Jesus is in the Qur'an, so why the problem?"

Ami just stared at me. I couldn't read her face, so I tried once more to explain. "Listen. Jesus told me that he would protect me. He knew I would be in danger. How can I not trust him now when he is the only one who saw what was going to happen to me and is the only one stepping in to protect me?"

Ami exhaled. She looked tired, and when she spoke, the words fell heavy from her mouth as if they were stars falling from the sky. "Nomi, if you tell people that, they will kill you."

Frustration surged up within me. "You don't understand! He's going to protect me. He won't let people harm me—he told me that when I was in England. I had a vision and then a dream, and God and Jesus told me that I was going to be okay!"

A flash of irritation swept across her face. "What about us though? Will he protect us as well?"

I didn't reply, because I didn't know the answer myself.

Things continued like this over the next few days. Most of the time our discussions ended with Baba-jan slamming the door or Ami taking a deep breath and telling me to go and rest. Sharib vanished from my life, and none of my friends made contact. My days became small, made up of sleeping and eating and going to school and visiting the roof where I prayed short, urgent prayers asking Jesus to help me.

I had started back at school after a week of being at home, just in time to finish the academic year. Baba-jan made it clear that I was not going to return to the Catholic school, and despite my protests he insisted that I use a different name and join an Islamic school on the other side of the city. I did as he said and attended my classes. Though Ami told me that news of what had happened to me had made it into the newspaper, either my picture had not been published or nobody at my new school had read it. Either way, everybody treated me as the new quiet kid. I went through my classes as if invisible, and I didn't mind at all.

I never felt alone as I rode my motorbike to and from my new school or walked through crowded corridors or across empty courtyards. The words of Jesus had a strange power about them and I remembered them often, carrying them with me like a stone in my pocket. They were like medicine to me, and I imagined that just by recalling his words I was somehow getting stronger. Stronger and less afraid.

I was riding home one day when I considered paying a visit to Uncle Faizal's. Both Ami and Baba-jan had been clear that I was not to go there at all, but I thought they were overreacting. The way that people ignored me at my new school had boosted my confidence— surely no one had really read about me in the newspaper. Things had been shaken up, yes, but surely they would settle again as before. I made a sudden left turn down a quiet road and felt like I was about to make a small gain in the battle for my life. If I could show my friends that I was still normal, that they had nothing to fear from me, then perhaps it would all blow away and we could return to life as normal.

I was enjoying this daydream as I braked behind a line of cars, waiting to pull out at a busy intersection a few streets from Uncle Faizal's, when I heard someone shout.

"Kafir!"

I swung my head around, trying to locate the sound. There, on the other side of the street outside a café, I saw them.

Yazie and a few other boys from my old school were running toward me. Panicking, I pulled on the throttle, the angry cries of my engine cutting through the noise of the surrounding traffic. I tried to edge forward, but the cars were thick like fog all around me. I revved louder, hoping to provoke the cars around me to move, but it was no use. All I could do was inch forward slowly. I looked back to see Yazie and the others gaining fast, just a few cars away now. I shouted for drivers to move, and when the smallest possible gap opened up, I shot my bike through like an arrow. I was almost at the intersection, but I was out of time. Their hands were on me, pulling at my jacket, trying to pull me down off the bike. I let go of the throttle to fight them off, and the sound of my bike was drowned out by the noise of their shouts.

The street was busy enough with other people for a small crowd to form around me. Even though Yazie and the others were calling me *kafir*, several older men in the crowd came to my defense, pushing the boys back.

As soon as I could, I roared away through the crowd, riding home as fast as I could. I was afraid to look over my shoulder the whole way. When I had recovered my breath enough to tell Ami part of the story—leaving out the bit about me being on my way to Uncle Faizal's—she held me and told me not to worry. I could feel her heart beating hard within her chest.

Baba-jan did not try to cover up his anger. "You are stupid," he told me that night. "You are not living in a Christian country. These people will kill you."

His words echoed a deep, deep fear that I was trying desperately to suppress.

I wanted simple things again—playing with my dogs, winning games at the arcade, flying kites, and dreaming of my future as a businessman selling fast, shiny cars. I had been running from the truth that I could not have any of this now that I had chosen something better.

I tried to brush off Baba-jan's warnings just as I tried to deny my own concerns about my safety, but my voice sounded weak when I spoke. "What do you mean 'these people'? It is just Yazie and his cousins. They will get bored of me eventually."

Baba-jan scoffed, "The man who stabbed you was Wahhabi."

"I know," I said.

"He's not just any Wahhabi. He's with the terrorists, and so is Yazie's father. You remember the bombings, don't you? He's with *them*."

That was all I needed for my defenses to crumble. A tight wire clamped itself around my chest, squeezing to the point where I thought I might cry out. I knew about these terrorists. Everybody knew. They were brutal and fearsome. They were a child's nightmare made of flesh, blood, and steel.

"I thought they were mainly in the north," I said quietly.

"No. They are here as well."

It took hours for my chest to feel normal again, and I couldn't sleep even when it did. I worried that my stab wound was going to open up again and kept checking the thin bandages for blood. Though my heart felt like a volcano about to erupt, I did not bleed. The last thing I wanted the next morning was to go to school, and Ami didn't make a fuss when I told her that I was feeling unwell, so I spent the day at home. I tried to think about Jesus, but it was hard. I had new thoughts now—terrifying thoughts—crowding him out. I had seen the terrorists' work before, on the news and on the internet. I had seen the images of men with their throats slit, of burned-out cars, of execution lines.

That night I went to Misim's room, hoping that hearing him sleep deeply would help me to relax as well. I lay quietly, listening to the cars that passed from time to time, hearing the sound of the goats and cows as they busied themselves on the patch of land out back.

I was drifting when I heard the first shout.

"Kafir!"

It was a single voice at first, but loud. That meant it was close. My blood pounded. The rest of the house was silent, and I looked through the open bedroom door. There was darkness in the corridor, so Ami and Baba-jan must have gone to bed. I crept toward the window, wondering if I had imagined it, but before I made it, I heard the shout again.

Baba-jan appeared at the door, half dressed but completely awake.

"Get away from the window," he said before closing the door. I went back to sit by Misim. More shouts came, thick and fast now, and closer still. I heard the sound of them pounding on the iron gates out front, all shouts and fists and metal.

I could hear them clearly now. There must have been ten of them at least, if not more. "Send him out or we will burn the house!" Somewhere in the house one of the servants screamed. Soon Misim's door opened again, and in came Zainab and Ami. Baba-jan was behind them and locked the door before leaving the room. The light was on and Misim was still groggy.

"What is it?" he asked. Ami held him and rocked him back and forth. Then came a new sound. Gunshots.

Misim started to cry and Zainab buried herself in the blanket that Ami had wrapped around her shoulders.

At first I thought they were aiming at the house, but I heard no glass breaking. Were they firing into the air? Whatever they were doing, it wasn't good. "Jesus," I prayed silently, but I couldn't think what to say next.

Baba-jan came back into the room, bringing the servants with him. They looked stunned and fearful. "Come," he said to me, holding out his hand and fixing me with a stare I didn't dare refuse. He pulled me out by my arm, locking the door behind him again.

"What's happening?" I asked, but he didn't reply. He marched on ahead, down the stairs. My panic flipped into another gear, just as if someone had revved the engine on my bike. "No!" I cried, fearful that I was about to be thrown outside to the mob. "Where are you taking me?"

He had to pull me down the stairs by both arms, and I had no choice but to run to keep up with him. Once at the bottom, I planted my bare feet on the cold tiles and tried to stop him. He looked back at me. "I'm taking you out the back," he said.

I could hear the shouts even more clearly once we went outside through the rear door. They were still calling for me to come out, still saying they were going to burn the house down. I followed Baba-jan across the yard to the smaller gate at the back and the place where Ami always parked her car. It was here that I had buried his bullets a few years earlier, and for a moment I wondered whether he had brought me here to dig them up so that we could defend ourselves. Instead he opened the door of Ami's Honda and told me to get in.

He pulled away quietly, leaving his headlights off until he had crossed the patch of grass and was able to join the road that led away from our house. I tried to twist in my seat to see whether we were being followed, but I saw no other cars.

Baba-jan stared at the road as if it was littered with mines, and his eyes never went more than a second or two without flicking up and checking the rearview mirror. After we had been driving for a few minutes, he relaxed a little. "Where are we going?" I asked.

"I don't know. Maybe I will take you to a hotel."

We drove some more, still in silence. I spent the whole time looking out the window, watching familiar streets pass by us, wondering all the time if every set of headlights we passed would spin around and mark the start of another attack.

Baba-jan suddenly swung a sharp turn onto the road leading out of Lahore. When I looked at him, he said, "We can't take you to a hotel. You'll get caught there. I'm taking you to my friend instead."

"Where?"

He mentioned Multan, a city two hours away. At first I felt comforted by the idea of getting away, but as the minutes and the miles passed, I started to wonder who this man was, what he was like, how long I would be staying with him. I was sixteen years old, but I felt like I was six.

I knew I couldn't ask Baba-jan any more questions, so I tried to keep myself distracted with memories of my trip to England. I drifted to sleep at some point and woke up when Baba-jan shook my leg. "We're here," he said. "Come on."

It was four in the morning and dark outside the car, though there were enough streetlights for me to see that we were outside a low house on a road lined with trees. It looked nice, but alien. I had never been here before, and when the door opened as soon as Baba-jan knocked, the man on the other side was a total stranger to me.

He held the door open and ushered us both in.

"What is this about, Manzoor? Your call worried me."

"It is nothing much, Hassan," said Baba-jan, suddenly looking more relaxed and good humored than I had seen him in weeks. "Ali here just got in a bit of trouble with some Wahhabi. I just need you to keep him for a few weeks until I can find somewhere else for him to go."

"Okay," said the man. "That's fine."

And that was it. Baba-jan stood up to leave and looked at me. "I have to go back and make sure they are okay."

I nodded. "Goodbye," I said. There was nothing else to say.

And if I wasn't sure before, I certainly knew now. There was no turning back.

CHAPTER 12

BLOOD
BECAUSE OF ME

"This is the way the world ends . . . not with a bang but with a whimper."
Years later I read those words in a poem by T. S. Eliot, but if I had come
across them as life with Hassan unfolded, I would have lain down on
the floor and wept. Piece by piece I was watching my life erode.

Hassan left the house every morning to go to his job as a cook in
a hotel restaurant, not returning until late at night. He had no family
living with him, and none nearby as far as I could tell. He kept no servants and had no visitors. I spent most of my waking hours alone, and
instead of feeling safe and calm as though I was so well hidden that
nobody on earth could find me, I began to feel my hope evaporate.

Left to myself and my fears, I sought solace and relief on the screen.
Hassan lived like a true bachelor and had an impressive range of video
games and consoles. Yet improving my high scores was only ever a
temporary distraction. Most of the time I thought about home. I tried
phoning the house most days but never received any reply. At first this
worried me, and I panicked a little until Hassan told me that he had
spoken to Baba-jan already and that he and the rest of the family had
left the big house for a while and made an extended visit to some of his
relatives in the country.

"It must have been bad for the whole of your family to have to leave like that," said Hassan. I knew he wanted me to tell him more, but I remembered Baba-jan's words from the night we arrived.

"It was just the Wahhabi," I said. "Nothing serious."

I had to trust that everyone was safe, but not being able to talk to Ami or the others myself created an awkward feeling within me, as if I had swallowed a stone. About the only time I was able to forget about it was when I was playing video games, but even their power to numb me began to wear off after a while.

Sometimes, if I was feeling particularly bored or brave, I would step out of the front door and go for a walk. At first I stuck to the tree-lined roads around Hassan's house, but after I had been living at his home for three weeks, I was confident enough to catch the bus into the heart of the city.

Multan was big, almost as big as Lahore and with plenty of sights and sounds to steal my attention. I spent so much time standing around, staring at businessmen and tourists, beggars and schoolkids, that I started to feel invisible. I had done much the same thing back in England, and there were times in Multan when I felt just as different from the world around me as I had on the streets of Oxford.

I liked feeling invisible like this because I wanted to put everything behind me. From the moment that the crowd had come to the house at night and demanded for me to be sent out, I had been hoping the turmoil would die down. I wanted to be allowed to return to life as usual, and I wasn't ready to give up my hope of things going back to normal just yet.

Yet I couldn't forget what had happened to me in England as well as after I had been stabbed. My dream and my visions were real, and I could still remember what it felt like to have the hairs on the back of my neck bristling from seeing Jesus.

The trouble was that every time I thought back to my encounter, I felt the gap between me and my family widen. So my prayers, such as they were, were short. Whenever I asked God for help, I was asking him to put everything back together just as it had been. I knew it was a foolish request. But still I prayed.

There were times in Multan when I started to doubt why I had said what I did to Yazie and the others. I began to question whether I really was a Christian. After all, I didn't yet own a Bible, had never been to church in Pakistan, and knew no other Christians to speak of. Why had I put myself at risk in order to defend Jesus like that? Was he really worth it?

Yet whenever I remembered how I told my friends about Jesus as we sat in front of the school, I remembered how I'd felt as though my insides were suddenly lighter and the air suddenly sweeter. I'd felt the same way when Aunt Gulshan first prayed for me, as well as when I'd seen and dreamed of Jesus.

The strangest thing of all was that just by remembering these moments, I found myself feeling stronger, less scared, and almost a little powerful. And when I felt like that, I no longer wanted to forget what had happened. I wanted to revisit it again and again, reminding myself that Jesus had done exactly as he said he would do, protecting me from harm. Perhaps he had even caused me to start talking about him in the first place.

Baba-jan had given me no idea how long I would be at Hassan's, but after four weeks I was beginning to know the city well enough to be able to navigate my way around without having to ask for help. Late one afternoon I was on one of my trips, passing by a large mosque on the way to a café half a mile away that I had discovered some days earlier. I was weaving through the crowds, thinking about the pomegranate juice I would order once I got there, when I heard wheels on the gravel road behind me. It was a large white SUV. Tinted windows—I couldn't see inside.

It kept pace with me even as I carefully picked my way across the busy street. Was it following me?

My nerves sparked and I wanted to run, but I checked myself.

What were the chances of my being able to outrun a car? A better plan was to get to the café and wait there for a while. Maybe I could phone Hassan too and see if he could come pick me up. So I willed my legs to keep steady and carried on walking.

The road was busy and the sidewalk just as crowded, but I still heard the SUV's engine growl and the brakes screech as a blur of white pulled up beside the sidewalk a few feet ahead of me. Before I could run, three men got out and grabbed my arms. They were all bigger than me, and each was at least ten years older than me. They were wearing dark *shalwar kameez*, all three of them had beards, and one wore a black turban. I knew instantly that they were Wahhabi.

"*Jaldi, jaldi,*" they said, speaking Punjabi. "Let's go!" I shouted for help, but this time no concerned onlookers were prepared to come to my rescue. The crowds that had been flowing along the street just seconds before had faded. Now they had become like ghosts, unable or unwilling to stop my kidnappers.

I was pushed into the back of the car and wedged between two of the men. A fourth man was driving. I didn't recognize any of them. The smell of smoke made me gag, and the men on either side of me on the backseat were heavyset and had me pinned between them. The man in the turban was slimmer and a little younger, but I could tell he was in charge. When he glanced back at me from the front passenger seat, I felt the same terror that had accompanied the sight of the switchblade.

The vehicle swerved away as soon as I was in, and the driver threw us all from side to side as he took corners faster than he needed to, causing a chorus of squealing brakes and angry car horns from the interrupted traffic.

"Where are we going to take him?" said the passenger in the front. His question prompted a long and loud discussion among all of the men, with some wanting to take me all the way back to Lahore while the driver wanted to deal with me in Multan.

I was feeling sick from the speed and the smoke and the fear, and watched in horror as a truck pulled out of a side road up ahead without looking both ways across the intersection. The SUV driver pumped the brakes and we skidded, pulling up just short of the truck, whose driver threw open his door and started shouting wildly at our driver. He pounded his fist and marched toward us. His rage sparked something in the men who had captured me, and everyone except the driver leaped out to confront the truck driver. On either side of me were open doors and empty seats. I didn't hesitate to scramble across them and run.

I knew I'd be faster on foot than the two burly men who had sat beside me, but I wasn't so sure about the other passenger. I sprinted back down the road, back in the direction of the mosque, running in the road whenever the sidewalk was too crowded. I heard the SUV's doors slam and the engine roar again, and made a sharp turn onto an even busier street where, to my relief, I saw a crowd of people wedging themselves onto a bus. I joined them, handed over my money, and willed the driver to pull away quickly and never stop.

Sitting in an aisle seat, I caught my breath eventually and gradually felt my heart return to something like normal. My wound was almost healed now, but it was still tender to the touch and I still worried when I got out of breath. It was foolish, but I often had visions of the scar opening up again whenever I felt my heart beat faster than normal. When the bus stopped for the last time and the final passengers exited, I climbed down as well. We were at a train station, though I didn't recognize the name. I needed to get back to Hassan's house, but the two rupees in my pocket weren't going to get me there. I found a guard and asked him for help.

"I have been out shopping and lost my money. I need to get home. Can you call me a taxi?"

"Why don't you call one yourself?"

"None of them will stop for me."

"Where are you from? Your accent's funny."

I was getting frustrated with him, but I knew I had no other options.

"I'm from Lahore and I'm visiting my father's friend. I just took the wrong bus and ended up here. Please, can you help me?"

The guard thought a while longer, his face not giving anything away. Eventually he gave in and told me to follow him to a taxi rank. "This is my nephew," he said to the first driver in the line, placing his hand on my shoulder. "Can you take him where he wants to go? He will pay you when he gets there."

The taxi driver shrugged and told me to get in.

"Thank you," I said to the guard.

"Look after yourself," he said. "Be safe." He paused. "And don't get involved in drugs."

As soon as we pulled up on the street outside Hassan's house, I could tell that his front door was broken. Inside everything had been smashed. The fridge was on the floor, his TV too. The gaming consoles looked as though they had been hurled against the wall. I stood in silence, taking it all in until Hassan came in from the yard out back, holding a brush and an old sack. His face turned ugly with anger.

"You and your father lied to me," he said. "You said it was just a small fight, but look at this. This is not what happens when it's nothing serious. They phoned me while they were still here and told me that I have twenty-four hours to hand you over or throw you out. If I let you stay here, we're both dead. You understand?"

I nodded. "I need to pay the taxi," I said quietly.

Hassan spread his hands wide. "Okay," he said. "Okay."

Three hours later Baba-jan pulled up outside the café that Hassan had told him to meet us at. "I want to help, but this is too much," Hassan said as he leaned in through the car's open window to say goodbye. "I have a job here and I can't keep Ali safe from them."

"I understand," said Baba-jan. "Thank you."

I waved goodbye and mouthed my thanks.

The drive out of Multan was slow. Traffic in the city was heavy and I found it hard to contain my frustration. I wanted to be free and safe, but Baba-jan was determined not to drive recklessly. "Calm yourself," he said as I twitched in the front seat, turning around every few seconds to see whether we were being followed. I had to fight the urge to shout at him in reply. I tried to distract myself by looking at the passengers in the cars surrounding us, but whenever I saw a white car, I panicked and hid down low in the seat. I knew it wasn't the same one the kidnappers had driven, but my nerves were a mess.

"Where are we going?" I asked once we finally pulled clear of the city and made it out onto a fast, wide road.

"Gujranwala."

I knew it. I hadn't been there for a long time, but an aunt lived there and I had happy memories of her looking after me during long summers before Ami and Baba-jan married. Aunt Nazia had always treated me kindly, and I hoped it was to her that Baba-jan was taking me. I didn't ask, though. I didn't want to be disappointed.

The drive was long, lasting more than a whole night. Baba-jan didn't want to talk much, so I willed myself to sleep as often as I could. When the morning came and we stopped for fuel and food, he finally asked the question. "What happened?"

I had already told him about the men in the SUV when he had met Hassan and me at the café, and I went over the details again. He wanted me to describe the car again in detail, as well as the men themselves.

"You're sure that you had not seen them before?"

"Yes, I am sure. I didn't recognize their accents either." Baba-jan looked thoughtful, as if he was trying to solve a puzzle. I wondered for a moment whether he might be on to something and let myself become momentarily lost in the idea that he might find a way for me to return. What he said next brought me painfully back down to reality.

"They won't give up, you know." I knew who he was talking about, but looked blankly back at him anyway. "They want you dead. This isn't just about Yazie's family or men from our neighborhood. The news of what you did must have spread, and they will send more people to hunt for you. All we can do is hide you and hope that we can move you to the next place before they find you again."

We got back in the car soon after and carried on driving. I felt like I had left my stomach back by the side of the road, as if I could never eat again. The thought of having these terrorists after me was too much. I had once seen a news report that explained how they had stopped a bus carrying Shia pilgrims, forced them to kneel on the side of the road, and shot them all point-blank. I could still picture the way the blood mixed with dust on the lifeless faces of their victims. And if being a Shia wasn't enough, I was also an infidel, a *kafir*, a traitor to Islam. I couldn't have given them any more reason to want me dead. I wondered how long I would last.

"What is going on with Ami and the rest of you?" I asked. "How come you don't answer the phone anymore?"

"We had to leave the house."

"Will you go back?"

"Inshallah."

I considered this. "If God wills," he had said. Did he? Did God really want my family to return home? Would he protect them too, even though they wouldn't allow their son to talk about his own Son, Jesus? And what God was Baba-jan talking about anyway? Was the God of Islam the same as the God of the Bible? I tried to wrestle with the questions, but it was all too much. The lack of answers made me weary.

By the time we made it to the outskirts of Gujranwala, the sun was already high enough in the sky to make the air hot and sticky. Baba-jan drove us through the midmorning crowds to a small house near a train station.

"Do you remember Aunt Nazia?" he asked.

"Yes," I said, relief flowing through me.

She was just as I remembered her. Eyes as big as precious stones and a smile that was enough to make me forget the aches that came from the night-long drive. She moved gently, like a dancer, her limbs flowing evenly as she scooped a little child and welcomed us in. She offered us tea and a comfortable chair to sit on, and I felt myself relax even more. Aunt Nazia was the youngest of Ami's cousins and wasn't much more than a decade older than me. She had twin small children now, a boy and a girl, and the way she let them hide behind her legs and gently encouraged them to come and greet the visitors reminded me of the way Ami was with Misim.

I guessed that Baba-jan had already told her about why I was here, but she didn't ask any questions. She simply offered us more tea, asked about the drive and the family back home, and encouraged the twins to show us their favorite toys.

Soon after we arrived, Nazia's husband came into the house and greeted us. Saaed was not much taller than me, and he had the same smile that Nazia did. I instantly felt at home there, and when Baba-jan left a few hours later, I told him to tell Ami that I was happy with the move. In truth, I was worried about getting caught again and didn't like the fact that Baba-jan was unwilling to tell me how long I would be there, but I didn't want to cause Ami to worry.

Saaed owned a number of small stores, and each day he visited each one in turn. The shops that had video games were my favorite, and I even managed to find one with a Tekken machine deep in the back. Saaed let me play while he collected the money from the tills, talked to the staff, and made sure everything was running smoothly.

Back at home I played with the twins, Iqbal and Umar, teaching Umar the best way to catch a cricket ball and helping Iqbal with her first attempts at reading. I missed Misim all the more for my time with the children. But at the same time, it was comforting to be with a family again.

When Saaed and I drove from store to store, we often talked. He never asked too many questions about what happened to me, and the conversation stayed focused mostly on my future. I told him I wanted to have my own business and that I'd been thinking about developing property.

"It is a good idea, but you will have to complete your education, won't you?"

"I know." I had been in my final year of high school when the first attack happened, and I hadn't been to school at all when I was staying with Hassan. If Gujranwala was going to be my home for the next few months, I knew I would need to resume my studies. "I'd rather just learn from you though," I said. "I could be your assistant and you could teach me everything about running a business."

Saaed smiled and told me that it was a good idea, "but not as good an idea as having your basic qualifications. Get back to school and you can still help me in the evenings and on weekends. I will be happy to have you around."

I did what he said and found a school. It was close enough to one of his stores for me to meet Saaed there each afternoon and accompany him on the last few visits each day, and though I was quiet among my peers, I liked the place well enough. After a month with Hassan and a month in Gujranwala, it was good to be back in a routine, especially since it distracted me from the danger I was running from. More than anything, I just wanted to be a normal sixteen-year-old again.

But that normalcy would always be fragile for me, and one day it shattered.

At the end of my third week at the school, Saaed and I were on our way home. We'd seen our usual shops, and as we drove, our conversation had covered a range of topics as diverse as stockholding, how to deal with dishonest employees, and why Honda motorbikes were better than any other make on the planet. We parked in the driveway and walked up to the house. I don't know if Saaed spotted the way the door was slightly open, but I did. A familiar feeling of terror clamped around my chest. I froze and watched him walk in.

His shout was loud enough to be heard from the street. It broke my paralysis and I ran inside after him. Door frames were stabbed with splinters and there was glass everywhere. Saaed continued to shout, and I followed his noise upstairs to one of the bedrooms.

He was kneeling on the floor, surrounded by broken furniture and scattered clothes, cradling Nazia's head in his lap. She was awake, but just, and lying awkwardly on her side. There was blood on her face and blood on her waist.

Iqbal and Umar were there too, holding on to their father as he wailed over his wife. They were crying too, but a different sort of cry. While Saaed was full of rage, the children were pinned to the floor by fear. As for me, I had no idea what to do. It was as if I had just arrived in my body, and everything in this world was strange and dangerous to me.

Saaed lifted Nazia and carried her down the stairs and into the car. He told me to bring the children and I sat with them in the backseat. Nazia was slumped in front with the seat laid flat, though I could not bear to look at her.

It should have been me, I couldn't help thinking. I was the one they had come for.

In the hospital I took charge of the children as much as I could, but they didn't want to lose sight of their father. So I waited and I prayed. I begged Jesus to protect Nazia and heal her just as he had healed me. I sat out front alone, rocking back and forth. I made bargains with God, pleading with him to save my aunt and prayed until I couldn't think of any new words to pray.

When it was dark outside, Saaed found me. He looked old and there was blood on his shirt. He stood in front of me and I didn't know whether I should stand or stay seated. When he spoke, his voice was unnaturally quiet, as if he was trying with all he had to keep it that way.

"She said that the men were looking for you. She said that she didn't tell them where you were and then they beat her."

I tried to stand. "Is she okay?"

In Saaed's eyes I saw the force of his anger. "This is all your fault," he said before turning around and walking back into the bright lights of the hospital.

I phoned Baba-jan as soon as I got back to the house and left a message on his cell phone. "You need to pick me up," I said. "It has happened again."

I tried to tidy the house as best I could. Partly I wanted to try to make amends for what had happened, but also it helped to be distracted. Even so, every passing car set my heart pounding again, and when I finally heard a key in the lock the next morning, I hid behind a door until I heard Saeed's voice telling the children to go and wash their hands. His voice was quiet now, as though he was using all his effort to make any sound in the first place.

I came out from my hiding place and waited until he walked into the room and found me. When he did, he stared at me. I couldn't look him in the face, so I looked at the floor. At the shards of glass still everywhere.

"She died," Saaed said. "Today I must bury her."

With that he left the room. I heard him pick up the phone and make the first of many calls, telling people that Nazia was dead and that the funeral would be before sunset. Though the words he used were the same with each call, the pain in his voice grew sharper with every one.

It took two days for Baba-jan to arrive. I kept myself away from Saaed, the children, and the increasing number of guests who filled the house. I tidied what I could and hoped Saaed wouldn't tell anyone of the part I played in the tragedy. I don't think he did, but the force of his grief was so strong that by the time I left, he was barely able to talk at all.

I was watching for Baba-jan's car, and when I saw it pull up out front, I quietly left the house. Baba-jan wanted to go in and pay his respects, but I stayed in the car. I had already brought too much pain into that one house.

We drove in silence for hours.

And for every mile we passed, I wondered if my choice was worth it.

CHAPTER 13

THE FOREST
OF FEAR

The drive from Gujranwala was long. This time it was my turn to be silent while Baba-jan's anger twisted within him, setting free his tongue to remind me that all of this was my fault.

"Haven't we given you enough? Even before you came back from England, you had everything you asked for. You had clothes and money and animals, and we bought you a motorbike. We sent you to the best school and took you to the best country club. You had everything from us, more than any other boy your age. So why wasn't that enough? Why do we now have to give up our homes for you? Do we all have to give our lives to protect you?"

I closed my eyes and tried to concentrate on the way the glass felt against my head. I focused on how cold it was, how I could feel the vibrations all the way down my back. For a while I was numb to everything else. But this lasted only a few miles, and soon enough the feelings of remorse came back.

Everything that Baba-jan said was right. Even before I left Hassan's house, I knew that my words and actions had already caused far too much pain and asked far too much of people. But now that Hassan had been exposed to the Wahhabi and Saaed had been robbed of his wife and his children of their mother, I didn't need to be reminded of how guilty I should feel.

I sat in silence for as long as I could, weighing the words that had been building within me for weeks. Finally, I let them out: "Take me home. I want to tell people that it was just a joke."

I had been thinking about those words for such a long time. I wished I had said them sooner. I had considered saying them on the drive from Multan up north to Gujranwala a month earlier, but the prospect of being taken to the safety of Aunt Nazia's home was too enticing. My hope was still intact then. If only I had spoken up, things would have been so different. If only I had taken back what I had said to Yazie and the others, then Aunt Nazia would still be alive.

I wanted to trust Jesus. I wanted to believe that he would protect me. But I wasn't so sure—not now, after all this loss. My faith in him had cost me too much. I wanted to turn back time, to bring Aunt Nazia back, to be with my family again.

Baba-jan stared ahead at the road, his hands tight on the wheel. I wondered whether he had heard me, so I said it again. "If you take me home, I will do what you want and tell people that it was just a joke."

He let out a cold laugh. "It is too late for that. The night they came to our house, it was too late for you to apologize and pretend that all this was just some joke. Now they want you dead and our family shamed. Nothing else will satisfy them."

I looked back at the road ahead, rested my head on the glass, dug my nails into my palms so hard that I hoped I would break the skin. But nothing could distract me from the chaos that raged inside me. It was as if all the fear, sorrow, and pain I had felt up to then had returned. I hunched forward and wept.

We drove through the night. In time the tears stopped and the chaos subsided a little, but I found no peace at all on that drive, and Baba-jan had no comfort to offer.

We passed a sign that said "India." "Where are we going?" I asked. I didn't care too much what the answer was, and I asked more because I wanted to puncture the silence than to find out where. Baba-jan mumbled something in reply and I didn't bother asking him to repeat it. Wherever it was, I assumed it would only be a matter of time before they found me. I would escape again, or perhaps this time they would catch me.

Late in the afternoon we turned off the fast road onto a smaller one that led into a forest. Our journey was slower now, but we didn't seem any closer to our destination. Mile after mile we carried on, through thick armies of trees, seeing the occasional person at the side of the road. I didn't bother asking Baba-jan where we were or what was going to happen next.

Another turn took us onto a thin dirt track. This one snaked its way through the trees, skirting around the bigger ones. We weren't driving much faster than walking pace by now, and the trees got thicker and the light got weaker the longer we drove. I stopped looking eventually and closed my eyes.

When the car finally stopped, I looked up. We had pulled up outside a small shack. The sun was starting to set, but I could see the bricks were made of clay and the roof made of tin, though both were battered, broken, with more than a few holes. There was one small window in the shack and a wooden door that had once been painted green. It had a padlock on it, but the door looked so old that I wondered what the point of locking it was.

I followed Baba-jan inside. The room was smaller than some of the bathrooms at home. A single bulb hung from the ceiling, its harsh light revealing the true state of the room. There was a battered old *charpai* crouched on the floor, its strings that crossed the frame were frayed and patchy. A tap in the corner sat above a dirty plastic bucket. Baba-jan crossed the room and tried the TV that was covered in dust, but it remained stubbornly silent. I saw one plate, one cup, and one basin to wash in.

"The toilet is out the back," said Baba-jan, wincing a little at the smell of stale breath and damp bricks that clung to the air. I looked at the dirt floor and remembered the white tiles we had at home, corridors so long that Misim and I could skate up and down them for hours.

Baba-jan stepped out the door again and went to the car. He opened the trunk and handed me a box. Inside were a few tins of food, some toothpaste and a toothbrush, and an old *shalwar kameez* that I always hated wearing. "There is a shop twenty minutes back down the track. Go there if you run out of food, but don't get into any conversations with anyone. Wear the *shalwar kameez* and only ever speak Punjabi. And if someone asks what you're doing here, just say you're working on the land. You understand?"

I nodded. It was a lot to take in.

"Only ever go to the shop, Nomi, no further. If you make them suspicious, they'll probably think you've been kidnapped or are trying to escape from something. You don't want them thinking either of those things, do you?"

"No."

"I'll be back next week," he said, walking back to the car.

"You're going now?" I said, panicking. He didn't look at me.

"There's some money in the box," he said before closing the door and starting the engine.

I watched Baba-jan drive off. When the trees swallowed him, I listened to the sound of the engine fade. When that was gone too, I stood and waited. Slowly other sounds took the car's place. There were cicadas and birds whose names I didn't know. I went inside and closed the door behind me.

The light was bright and the room looked even worse as I stood there alone. I tried to make myself busy by going through the contents of the box, but Baba-jan had left nothing for me to discover for myself. There were tins of peaches and some dates, and a few bags of nuts and some rice. Other than the clothes, the toothbrush and toothpaste, and an envelope with fifty rupees in it, there was nothing else at all. No books, no pen and paper. No phone.

I heard an unfamiliar noise. It sounded like laughter from a child's nightmare and I jumped to my feet. I opened the door and heard it again, then a third time. I told myself it was just a bird, but my pounding chest refused to believe me. I stepped back in and found that I could fasten the padlock on the inside. That eased my mind a little, but when the light suddenly flickered out a few minutes later, I was hurled back into my state of panic again.

I sat in the corner, my knees hunched to my chest, the tins of food beside me in the hope that I might be able to use them as weapons if I had to. My breathing was rapid and shallow and I tried my best to slow it down, but every time I did, a new noise from outside—a strange grunt or a bark, or the noise of something tearing at the trees—would set me off again.

All night I sat like that, and by the time the sky turned from silver to pale gray, I was exhausted. I finally managed to sleep, but when I did my dreams were just as bad. I saw men smashing down doors, heard children screaming and cars speed up behind me, never letting me get away.

Fear was exhausting work.

When I woke up it was hot inside and bright out. The electricity was back on and the light was filling in the gaps between the sunlight that leaked in through the window and the gaps in the door, ceiling, and walls. My mouth was dry and my skin and clothes were sticky with sweat and dirt from the floor.

From where I sat I could see there was an old satchel underneath the *charpai*. I pulled it out hoping for something like a knife or a gun, but all I found was a set of old clothes that stank worse than the room itself.

I went out and sat on the ground again and watched. There were a few cows in the distance and some goats close by. Crows and ravens bickered in the trees, and I thought I could hear a dog bark in the distance. Baba-jan had never said anything about the shack in the past, and I guessed it was owned by a friend or business acquaintance of his. I tried to imagine the man who had stayed here before and left the satchel. Looking after the land and animals in a place like this was the work of someone far down the caste system, less than *umti*, even. And here I was, hoping that a place like this was remote enough to keep me alive.

I put on the *shalwar kameez* and ate some of the dried fruit that Baba-jan had left me. Around the back of the shack I discovered the pit toilet that he had mentioned. I walked a little farther into the forest, though like a newborn calf that never strays too far from the safety of its mother, I always made sure that I was close enough to see it.

After the fear that had kept me awake all night, I felt calmer that day. Yet I was troubled by the fact that I had no memory of passing by the shop that Baba-jan had mentioned. I tried to imagine what it would be like, hoping it might be like Uncle Faizal's, but images of murderous thugs sitting around drinking alcohol hovered at the edges of my mind.

I watched the cows and counted seven of them. I tried to entice one over toward me. It was black and brown, with its ribs starting to show. Like all the others it was slow and old, though the way her horns stretched back from her head gave her a majestic look. Just watching her graze along the forest floor calmed me, reminding me of the time that one of my *mureed* brought me my own cow. I wondered whether this one would ever allow me to drink her milk, but she looked as though she hadn't nursed a calf in years.

I decided that not knowing about the shop was worse than having to face any drunken thugs who were there, so when the sun started to drop a little in the sky, I picked up the envelope with the rupees, padlocked the shack, and started in the direction that Baba-jan had left the night before.

It was farther than I imagined, and soon the road had twisted this way and that so much that I had no idea which direction the shack was in. I tried to memorize distinctive trees and kept an eye out for any sign that the shop might be close. It was only when the track joined another, wider track, of which I had no memory at all, that I saw it.

The shop wasn't much of a shop. It was perhaps twice the size of my shack, with four *charpais* out front sitting on either side of a couple of low wooden tables. There were a few oranges stacked on bricks, and a man sitting on a straw mat hacking up some meat and throwing it in a pot, and that was it. I saw a television inside. At least it was working.

I sat on one of the *charpais* and asked for some food and tea. The drink was sweet and the meat and rice I was given was good. I watched the TV through an open door and started to feel a little better. I thought about trying to make conversation with the man cutting up the meat, but Baba-jan's words of warning rang loud in my head. As the sun started to drop, I left.

My second night at the shack was even worse than the first. My trip to the shop had occupied my thoughts all afternoon, and the return walk had been a further distraction as I checked off the trees that I had tried to remember on the way there. But once I was back, there was no way to ignore what I knew was coming. I sat out front watching as the last light drained from the sky, fighting the growing sense that I was about to choke on the stale air around me. And when it was finally dark, I ran inside, padlocked the door, and took up my place on the floor in the corner. I willed the electricity to stay on that night, but just like before, it died, leaving me alone in the darkness once again.

All night I sat, shaking and trying just to breathe. I'd close my eyes for a while, not in the hope of sleep, but to block out the strange shadows that the moonlight threw onto the wall. Then the sounds of foxes and owls and whatever else I could not identify would grow so loud in my mind that I would have to open my eyes again.

Hour after hour I sat like this, convinced that it was only seconds before my door would crash open and someone would arrive to carry me off. I searched the sky for signs that the sun might be rising, but none came and I wondered if time itself had left me.

"Jesus, I need your help. If it's really you, if you're really listening, I need you." I tried to pray. I remembered the words of Jesus and tried to make myself remember the feelings that had accompanied them, but though I could catch hold of them for a moment, a new or unexpected noise would startle me and the fear would take over again. All I was left with were the prayers of a frightened little boy. "Please help me! Please make it all go away!"

Finally, just when I was more exhausted than I ever thought possible, I saw the first signs of a lighter patch in the sky. I crept onto the edge of the *charpai*, drew my knees up close to my chest, and gave in to sleep.

And so my routine was set. Each day started the same way, with me opening my eyes to the daylight and trying to sweep from my mind the memory of the nightmares where men chased me and children cried for their dead mother. I would wash myself, wishing the tap and bowl were like the shower we had at home. The mornings were my favorite, as I sat outside and watched the animals move slowly about, never hurrying, never changing. At some point I would walk to the shop and order a plate of whatever they had cooked that day, which I always ate quickly. I'd then watch TV and sit around for as long as I could before ordering a second meal. This I savored, chewing each mouthful slowly, trying to concentrate on the flavor and texture. It wasn't that the meal was particularly good, but I was desperate to distract myself from the night that was about to begin.

When the sun started to dip, I paid and walked quickly back to the shack, counting the trees as I went and watching for snakes. I'd sit out front as long as I could, watching the birds as they had their last battles of the day. But when the light finally left and my heart was working faster than a steam train, I would run inside and hope that for once the hours might slip by a little faster. They never did.

Occasionally the man who cut the meat tried to talk to me. He asked me where I was from and what I was doing there, but I had rehearsed Baba-jan's lines so many times that the lie came easily to my lips. "My name is Khan," I said. "I am working on the land here."

One morning, a week or so after I arrived, I heard something unfamiliar as I sat watching the cows. It was a car, and judging by the sound it was coming up the track. I pulled the door shut and scrambled around the back of the shack, hiding behind a wide tree nearby. The sound grew louder and must have been close, but the trees were too thick for me to see. I thought about running but decided to stay and watch a while longer. If it was someone who had come to get me, I figured I could probably lose them quickly in the forest. And if I had been discovered, I wanted to be sure.

Just as the car cleared the last line of trees, I breathed out in relief. It was Baba-jan.

"Nomi," he said as he saw me walking toward him. *"Al-salamu alaykum."*

"Wa alaykum," I replied.

"How are you?"

"Well," I lied. "How is everyone?"

"Well."

"Did they not want to come with you?"

"The drive was too long for them," he lied.

Baba-jan stayed no longer than a few minutes, handing me some more money and fresh supplies of food. "I will return next week," he said.

As I watched his car disappear, I realized I hadn't asked him to bring me a flashlight or a phone. I sat back on the ground and felt the night start early. I was already dreading the dark.

The next week he came, just as he said he would, though this time he stayed a little longer. After the usual greetings and my asking about the family, he paused. "Sharia law says that an apostate can be held for three days and nights. During those days people are free to try to convert him back to Islam. If he still refuses, then they kill him."

I didn't know why he was telling me this, and Baba-jan must have noticed my confusion.

"I won't let them kill you, but I want you to be sure about what you are doing. Are you going to refuse Islam? Are you really going to turn your back on it?"

I didn't have an answer for him yet.

Two weeks earlier I would have told him no. But things were different now. I knew there was no way to appease the Wahhabi, no way to erase my name from their hit list. Life simply could not return to how it was. Nothing would ever be the same again.

Yet in the days that followed, I found myself drawn to prayer in ways I had not experienced since being back at home and taking refuge on the roof. My breath would grow heavy within me. It was as though time was slowing around me. I could remember what it felt like to be close to Jesus, and from somewhere I could always hear an echo of his words, telling me not to be afraid, reminding me that he would protect me.

I even started to have better dreams as I lay in the early morning sun. I dreamed I was happy and peaceful, that I was free from all this crippling fear.

I would wake from these dreams feeling deeply happy. I had never known so much fear before, but neither had I known such peace. Even though I had no Bible with me and knew so very little about Jesus, I could still remember the words of the Lord's Prayer that Aunt Gulshan had taught me the night I woke her up at her house in Oxford. I returned to the words as often as I could, often when I was running back from the shop, resisting the fear crouching behind every tree. I knew that the words were powerful, and with each journey back I was adding to a growing belief that the more I prayed, the safer I felt.

Certain phrases in the prayer stood out to me. Calling God "Father" was still a revolutionary change from years of Islam, where Allah was to be feared and revered, not approached like a loving parent. I liked praying, "Thy kingdom come," too, for I felt that just by saying the words I was playing my part in speeding up the end of the world, the restoration of all things. I had never imagined it this way before. I'd always believed that the world would end with earthquakes and tremors and darkened skies and destruction for all but the most faithful few. I had a far clearer picture of hell than I did of heaven.

The terrors of hell always felt closer to me at nighttime. No matter how well I slept at dawn and no matter how good I felt when I prayed during the day, the noises and darkness closed in at night just the same.

And as I entered my third week in the shack, I found myself spending more and more time imagining what Ami, Zainab, Misim, and Baba-jan were doing. I tried to picture what their new home would look like, what trees would be giving shade in their courtyard, and how Misim would be coping at his new school. Sometimes these thoughts made me cry so hard I wondered if I was going to be able to find the next breath.

The third time that Baba-jan visited, I was ready to talk. Nervous, but ready. "I am not a Muslim anymore," I said. "I cannot go back." I knew that part of my life was now closed. Ahead of me was a strange new journey, full of mystery and the unknown. But I knew for sure that I could never worship as a Muslim again.

He just looked at me, staring as if trying to weigh the truth of my statement. "I sold your bike," he said eventually, speaking as if he were telling me about the weather. "I had to do it. We're trying to convince everyone that you have disappeared and that we don't know where you are, and keeping your bike was starting to look suspicious. So I sold it. I got twenty-five thousand rupees for it."

"I don't want the money. You can keep it."

"Very well," he said. Nothing about my decision seemed to anger him. He was perfectly calm, and that made me feel worse. I was being wiped out of my family's life and Baba-jan was not in any way upset about it.

"So are you going to sell the house as well? You're going to pretend I've disappeared? You're going to get rid of every bit of my inheritance?"

He just shrugged. The intense pain of missing my family rose up again, but this time it mutated. Twisting within me, it gave birth to anger. I hated what was happening. I wanted to rage at him, though I knew Baba-jan was the only person who was offering to help me.

"I don't want to talk to you." I turned and ran off into the forest.

The words of the Lord's Prayer returned to my mind as I kicked fallen logs and listened to Baba-jan drive away. One line stood out in particular: "Forgive us our sins as we forgive those who have sinned against us." I was able to say the words, and I knew they were important, but I had no experience of ever having to forgive anyone, and the concept was brand new to me. How could I forgive Baba-jan?

The next week, my fourth, Baba-jan's visit was less brief. He brought more food than usual and handed me an envelope with some of the money from my bike. I wasn't convinced by his friendliness. Something about it didn't add up.

"If you want me to talk to you, then you need to put Ami on the phone."

I didn't think he was going to let me talk to her, but he dialed and handed me his phone.

"Ami?" I said when she answered. She cried for the longest time, and I was weeping too, trying to tell her what I was feeling in between taking gasps of air. The only things to say were the things that really mattered. I told her I loved her, I missed her, and I wished she would come to see me sometime.

"Stay strong, Nomi," she said. "We will come and visit you soon enough."

When we said goodbye and I handed Baba-jan his phone back, he was holding some papers. "I need you to sign these," he said.

"Why?"

"I need to make people believe that you have gone and that you are not coming back."

I had no idea what I was signing, but I didn't care. I did what he wanted.

The next time I saw Baba-jan, only a few days had passed since I spoke to Ami. He looked excited as he climbed out of the car. "We are going to apply for you to go to England," he said, waving some paperwork and my passport in front of me. "Sign these and we can get you a visa."

I hadn't thought about this before, but it made sense. Baba-jan knew it too. "You can go live with Aunt Gulshan again. You can study there and gain some great qualifications. Then, perhaps after a year or two, you can come back."

I liked the idea, but not the thought of being apart from Ami, Misim, and Zainab for so long. Even being away from Baba-jan for two years would be hard, and in spite of all the anger I'd directed at him, I was grateful for all of the time he had spent rescuing me.

"I will go, but I want to go with my family."

"Of course," he said. "Of course you do."

He walked back to the car, holding the papers I had signed. "Next time I see you, I will bring everyone and take you to the airport. How does that sound?"

I smiled and watched him leave. If he was telling me the truth, then his plan could very well be the best solution for all of us.

CHAPTER 14

THE COURAGE TO FORGIVE

After the airport security doors glided shut and I came face-to-face with my tearstained reflection, I knew I had no option other than to walk away and prepare to board the plane. All my optimism about leaving Pakistan had drained away and taken the last of my strength with it. Ami, Misim, and Zainab were now barred from me, and I had nothing left within me to fight with.

I sat beside a nun reading a Bible as I waited for my flight to be called. It had been over a year and a half since I had been on a plane and exactly the same time since I had seen a Bible. As much as I was fascinated by its thin pages and dark, thick cover, I couldn't bring myself to start up a conversation with the Sister. What if she thought I was trying to trick her? What if someone saw me? What if she told the police?

I didn't want to get on the plane either. It was impossible for me to untangle the jumble of nerves inside, but I knew that somewhere among the fear of being caught by the Wahhabi, the fear of leaving my homeland, and the fear of how I was going to start again in England was the fear that I might just die on the plane itself.

I sat and stared at the black screen in front of me throughout the flight. When it came time to file off the plane and join the crowd waiting at passport control, I shuffled along with the line, so full of anxiety and exhaustion that I found it hard to think straight. When I handed over my passport and landing card, the officer said a few words I didn't understand and called over to a man with skin like mine.

"He says you haven't filled in the card correctly," he said, speaking Urdu with a heavy Indian accent. "What are you doing here? Where's your family? Are you traveling on your own?"

I didn't want to answer him. If I said the wrong thing, I was worried they might send me back to Pakistan, so I mumbled the minimum that I thought I could get away with.

"How long are you staying here?"

"Not long," I said. "I want to go back to Pakistan."

"You're here for your holidays?"

I pulled out my return ticket from my pocket and handed it over. "Yes," I said. "Just a holiday."

The officer looked between me and the ticket a few times, then stamped and returned my passport and wished me a good trip.

I knew nothing about claiming asylum, and nobody said anything to me about it. I didn't even know what it was or that it would have been possible to be allowed to stay in the country because of what had happened back home. All I knew was that until I made it through the doors and met Aunt Gulshan again, I was worried that at any point I was going to feel a pair of heavy hands on my shoulders and be told that I was going to have to return home right away.

When I finally saw her, Aunt Gulshan was exactly where she had been when Zainab and I had first arrived. This time Aunt Gulshan looked older, her face lined with worry, but as soon as she saw me, her old smile returned. Emily drove us back out to Oxford, and as I looked at the passing cars and spotted familiar landmarks, I began to feel just a little of my previous excitement return. *Perhaps this will be a new start,* I said to myself. Maybe I'd finally be safe here. Whether it was a few months or a couple of years, I began to wonder whether I might be able to make something good come out of it by picking up a good education and returning home a cultured, well-traveled young man, the kind people took seriously and treated with respect.

I knew it was a fantasy, but I needed something to distract me. It took Aunt Gulshan to help me see things clearly. We didn't talk much in the car, but once we arrived back at her house, she asked if she could see the scar from the stabbing. The wound had long since healed, but she drew in her breath as I showed her the dark scar that branded the side of my chest. I watched her eyes grow wider as I told her all about the Wahhabi, the vision of Jesus, and the terrible thing that had happened to Aunt Nazia. When I finished, she was silent for a while.

"I had no idea," she said. "I thought that you had just been injured in a schoolyard fight. I didn't know that you had been attacked for following Jesus." She paused some more and I wondered whether she was thinking about Aunt Nazia, who was one of her nieces.

I woke up the next morning to the sound of an unfamiliar voice downstairs. It took me half an hour to summon the courage to go downstairs and say hello, but as soon as I did, I was glad.

"This is Natasha," said Emily, pointing to a girl a few years older than me. She was taller too, and though she looked like she was Pakistani, she both dressed and held herself more as Western girls did. She was confident, relaxed. I liked her straightaway.

"Do you want to come to church with me?" she asked in Urdu.

"Sure," I said.

We walked to the meeting in the center of town, and as we did Natasha told me about her own background. She had converted from Islam to Christianity and had made her home here in Oxford and found a job. If ever there was a person I needed to talk to that day, it was Natasha.

I hadn't been to her church before, and though it was big and I struggled to understand what was being said by everyone, I felt as though I could belong there. Just as we were getting ready to leave at the end of the service, Natasha told me she had someone she wanted me to meet. One of the men who had been leading came over, a broad smile on his face and his hand outstretched toward me. He was slim and smartly dressed, neat gray hair combed back perfectly. I liked him instantly.

"*Al-salamu alaykum*," he said.

"*Wa alaykum*," I replied, feeling momentarily surprised at hearing such familiar language here.

"My name is Gordon," he said. "Welcome to the family."

Family—I didn't know what the word meant anymore, but I knew I wanted to be part of it.

The rest of the day saw me lost in a new daydream as a part of me came alive to the idea that the journey ahead of me might not be so bad after all. If I could follow Natasha's footsteps and find my place in the church, then maybe everything would work out all right.

The daydream vanished once night fell. As soon as I was asleep, I heard *mullahs* pounding at my door, saw them waving knives and heard them calling for my blood. I woke up, confused by the darkness, trying to remember where I was. I held my breath so I could listen for any sign of life in the house. I propped a chair against the door and hoped that when I drifted off to sleep again I would dream of better things. I did not get my wish.

It was Natasha who suggested that I apply for asylum. Aunt Gulshan hadn't needed protecting from family back in Pakistan, but Natasha's experience was closer to mine and she knew that without permission from the UK Home Office, I would have to return to Pakistan in six months, once my tourist visa expired.

And so I found myself seated in the office of a lawyer in London. The man on the other side of the empty desk was Indian, a Hindu, who spoke Urdu. Sitting next to Aunt Gulshan and Emily, I was smiling, looking forward to hearing him explain everything he was going to do to make sure I would be granted asylum by the good people of the United Kingdom.

"What do you know about Jesus?" His first question left me confused.

Why was he asking this? I still had a smile on my face, but as I looked at his stony expression, I felt all the excitement and anticipation begin to drain from my skin. "I . . . I know that he is the Son of God . . ." I stumbled. The lawyer made no movement or sound. "And I follow him and worship him?" I added.

The lawyer blinked. "What do you know about his disciples?"

I looked at Aunt Gulshan. "Did he have *mureed*?" She nodded. "I never knew," I said quietly. So far my faith had been based on two visions, one dream, and a man who had appeared to me, promising to protect me. I knew nothing about the Bible, nothing about Jesus, nothing about what a good Christian should be able to say if his life depended on a test of his faith. I felt suddenly exhausted, as if I hadn't slept the whole week since I had arrived.

"Perhaps you should read more of your Bible before you attend your interview with the Home Office," the lawyer said.

And so it took an Indian Hindu to show me, a Pakistani former Muslim, the importance of the Bible. As soon as we got home, Aunt Gulshan told me to sit down next to her. "We are going to start right now," she said, reaching for a copy of the Bible in Urdu. "And we will begin with the earliest story of them all."

I wish I could say that the scales fell from my eyes that night, or that I fell in love with Scripture. The truth is less simple. As Aunt Gulshan read about Adam and the garden, I remembered sitting with the *mullah* at home reading about Adam and his wife and how Allah taught Adam the names of the animals. I remembered the way the angels were commanded to bow down before Adam, but one of them, a *jinn* who tempted the first man and woman and became known as Shaitaan, refused to bow and was expelled from paradise. Adam and his wife were sent away too but were told that Allah would guide them.

Aunt Gulshan's story was different. The nameless wife from the

Qur'an was Eve, and Adam wasn't taught the names of the animals but chose them himself. No angels bowed down before Adam, and instead of forgiving him and his wife, God cursed them.

It made no sense to me. The story was so close, yet so very far.

"Very well," said Aunt Gulshan after I had thrown a hundred questions at her. "Let us start somewhere else."

Everything was different as we started to read about Jesus. I knew him already. All my powerful memories of hearing and feeling his voice flooded back over me as the description of his birth and first conversations with his earliest disciples filled the room. I could close my eyes and know exactly how Simon and Andrew, James and John felt to watch Jesus walk up to them and say, "Follow me." I read about Jesus casting out the *jinn*, and I knew what that felt like too. When he healed people who were sick, I remembered every moment that I lay dying on the hospital bed.

Reading about Jesus made all my previous frustration evaporate, but there was more to it than simply being able to understand the stories. The more Aunt Gulshan and I read of the New Testament, the more I knew this story was my own. Whenever I remembered how I felt about Allah, I was reminded of nothing more than fear—of the Wahhabi, of doing or saying the wrong thing in a mosque, of the *mullahs* with their twisted views of the world. I remembered pipe bombs and roadside executions, bloodied corpses and raging mobs. Yet whenever I thought about God, I could taste nothing but peace.

Finally I knew that I was not lying to myself. I had not been deceived. I was a follower of Christ and nobody could tell me otherwise.

By the time that Emily drove Natasha, Aunt Gulshan, and me back down to London for my meeting with the Home Office a week later, I was feeling confident. Even waiting three hours did not dampen my enthusiasm, and when I was finally called into a small interview room by a young woman with a kind face, I felt even better.

"Would you like your aunt to join us?" Everybody was so polite and gentle in England, not like they were back home. In Pakistan, even a Sayed like me could expect a government official to bark orders at me and make life as awkward as possible.

"I would like my aunt here, please. What's going to happen?" I asked, grateful for the interpreter who was also in the room.

"I'm just going to ask you a few questions. I'll take some notes, but I won't be making the decision. But you will hear from us soon. Within two or three weeks."

I turned to Aunt Gulshan as she was wheeled in beside me. "That's not long, is it? That's good."

The woman pointed to a dictating machine on the desk. "I'm going to record our interview."

"Can I have the recording?"

"Your solicitor will have to ask for it. Why do you want it?"

"Nobody has ever recorded me before!"

I was so happy to be there, glad that everything was in hand and being taken care of. I felt like I could trust the woman who was interviewing me, like she wanted to help, and for three hours I answered all her questions. She asked about my family, about my history, and all about the stabbing. She didn't want to see the wound but asked me whether I had any pictures that I could show her.

"No," I said. "I don't."

"That's okay," she said. "We're done." She told Aunt Gulshan to go back and wait with the others and showed me into another, larger room. There must have been ten desks arranged around the edge, each one with an officer seated at it. In the middle were chairs where I was told to wait. The air was no colder and the lighting no brighter in this room, but it was as if I had just walked into another world. Instead of gentle men and women talking politely to those around them, I watched as an older man started first to cry and then to shout before being pulled out of the room by guards.

Sitting there without Aunt Gulshan, Emily, Natasha, or even the man who had interpreted for me during my first interview, I could taste the bitter shock as it dried out my mouth. All along I had believed that I was in the company of people who wanted to help me stay in England, but for the first time I realized they also had the power to send me home.

I remembered the fear I had while living in the shack—primal fear, blinding fear—and I felt it rise again now.

I sat there for another thirty minutes, waiting until someone called my name. With every minute that passed, every raised voice I heard, and every fearful glance from the other interviewees, the terror within me rose. I became convinced that I was about to be thrown out and that within hours I'd be back at the airport waiting for a plane to take me back to the home in which I would surely be killed. I prayed, of course, but my words were too quiet and weak to drown out the fear.

Eventually I heard my name called and was motioned over to a desk. This time the officer made no attempt to be polite or gentle. He simply told me to sit still while he took my photo and showed me how to place my fingers on the ink pad in order to give my prints. I felt like a fraud and a common criminal but somehow managed to find the courage to ask him why he was doing this.

"For our records," he said, not looking up at me as he pushed his chair back, gathered a few forms, and walked away to a side door.

I waited. I sat, trying to wipe the ink off my fingertips with the single piece of tissue he'd given me. I wondered whether they would let me say goodbye to Aunt Gulshan or whether they would drag me out like they had the other man I had seen.

After ten minutes the man returned, sat at his desk, and asked for my passport. I didn't have the courage to ask why, but quietly removed it from the battered envelope that held the few papers I had brought with me.

In return he handed me something, saying, "This is your ID card. Don't lose it."

Did that mean I was in? I was desperate to know but couldn't be sure. I looked at the man and he spoke slowly, as if to a child. "When a decision has been made about your case, we will let you know and invite you back. Until then you cannot work and you cannot open a bank account."

And that was it. A minute later I was back with Aunt Gulshan, Emily, and Natasha. When they asked me what happened, all I could do was show them the ID card and say that I thought it went okay.

My solicitor told me it would take weeks before the Home Office reached a decision, and so I tried to put it all behind me and settled into life in Oxford. I had arrived in the country just after Easter, and as soon as the local college opened again, I took Natasha's advice and visited to find out about enrolling in some courses. The staff there told me it was too late in the year to start but that I could return and enroll in September. I didn't mind too much, as the idea of spending five months developing my newfound passion for basketball seemed like a good one. Besides, I was sure that by the time college started again, I would have been told that my appeal had been successful and I was allowed to stay.

I often took Aunt Gulshan with me, wheeling her in her chair and parking it at the side of the court. I never did see the boys who had been rude to me on the basketball court two summers earlier, but I did get to improve my jump shot. And when two girls, both about ten years older than me, walked onto the court one afternoon and asked if they could join me, I looked back to Aunt Gulshan, who smiled and waved me on.

Better than basketball and better even than the anticipation of a successful claim for asylum was church. Even though Easter had passed, there was still talk of Jesus' resurrection. It introduced me to a whole new side of the story that I was only vaguely familiar with. Gordon, the man I had met on my first visit, made a point of talking to me every Sunday, and soon I was meeting up with him at his office during the week. We talked about God and the Bible and Jesus and what it meant to be a Christian. We prayed too, and with every meeting I could feel my faith grow stronger and stronger. I realized that when

I left Pakistan I was like a tree that had grown tall very quickly, but whose roots were shallow. After a month in Oxford, I began to feel as though nothing could shake me.

Part of that was the result of another change within me. Before I left Pakistan for the first of my trips to England, I was full of confidence that my bright future was there for the taking. The months that followed had stripped nearly all of that attitude from me, and by the time I entered my third month in England, I was beginning to think that I was unlucky to the bone.

Yet instead of feeling anxious or depressed, I began to see as I continued to meet with Gordon that not being able to rely on my connections, my cultural standing, or my confidence was really a good thing. For the first time in my life, I was dependent on God. I was praying more and also praying differently. Where before my prayers were questions—"Jesus, is it really you?"—now my prayers were strengthening day by day, forming into certainties. When I prayed now, I fully expected God to hear me and to act.

"Jesus, I know you are real now," I prayed. "I know you can hear me and I know you can help. And I need you more than ever."

Gordon's first words to me, welcoming me to the family, were always in my mind during those first weeks at church. He introduced me to other people, and I took an instant liking to people like Tim—a kind man who spoke Urdu fluently—and Eddie, a younger man who told me that when I was ready I could join him when he went out to the Cowley Road, the heart of the city's large Pakistani community, and spoke to Muslims about Jesus. He smiled as he told me this, and though I wondered whether he might be joking, I knew inside that one day I would join him.

One morning as I sat down before the Sunday service started, I felt a quick tap on my shoulder and turned around to see a girl I recognized but couldn't place.

"Basketball?" she said.

"Yes!" I said, remembering her from the time we had played while Aunt Gulshan watched. "What are you doing here?"

"This is my church," she said.

"Mine too."

We talked about basketball and church and she introduced me to her fiancé and told me that if I ever wanted to join with them and the rest of the people from church who played every Tuesday, I would be welcome.

"I would like that," I said, hoping Aunt Gulshan would agree.

Everything about church was good. And so when Gordon suggested that I might like to get baptized, I agreed without hesitation. I knew nothing of the custom before reading about it in the Bible, but as soon as I had a mental image of John baptizing Jesus, I knew I wanted the same thing for myself. It felt so sacred. I wanted to belong, to know that I really was a member of a church. So my meetings with Gordon became even more frequent and I looked forward to every visit to his office in the church where I would learn more about what it meant to be a Christian. Even the times when I felt challenged by what he said were valuable.

"You need to forgive your father for abandoning you and mistreating your mother."

Gordon's words did not surprise me. I'd been thinking about how I might need to forgive Baba-jan since I had been in the forest, and somehow those thoughts had led me to start thinking about my real father. I knew Gordon was right, though his challenge raised more questions than answers within me. "If you want me to say that I forgive him, I will, but I might never see my father again for the rest of my life. If I can't see my father face-to-face, how can I forgive him?" I paused. "Gordon, what is forgiveness?"

"Well, it's not cheap," said Gordon. "It costs more than you might think you can pay, but with God's help you will be able to do it. And it's not a one-time event, either. You will find yourself needing to forgive them repeatedly. You do this by letting go—by giving up your anger, your bitterness, and your right to judge to God, who always deals justly in his time. Eventually, once you are able to see them or think about them and not feel full of bitterness or revenge, you will know that you've truly forgiven them."

We sat in silence for a while as I let his words sink deep.

"I like the idea of not feeling that way about my father," I said. I was still unsure what this meant, but I knew I wanted to try.

Things became clearer a few days later when Gordon and I next met and he asked me whether I knew who the Holy Spirit was.

"No," I said, and sat feeling increasingly confused as he told me about God taking on three different forms. "But I thought there was only one Jesus," I said. "Now you're telling me this? I am confused."

I felt better when we prayed and Gordon asked for the Holy Spirit to visit me in person. I felt the same light, peaceful feelings I felt when I was dreaming the first time and I listened as strange sounds came from my mouth, words in a language I hadn't heard before. When it was over, I knew I wanted to forgive my father for abandoning me.

"And what about the people who stabbed you?" said Gordon. "Will you forgive those people too?"

It was harder to forgive Yazie and his cousins, but I knew I needed to. I prayed for each of them, even the *mullah* who had stabbed me, and I spoke words of forgiveness out into the room. I hadn't even realized how heavy a weight I'd been carrying until I let it go.

When it came time for me to go home, I declined Gordon's offer of a lift and walked instead. I wanted to be alone, to hold on to the feeling of freedom and relief that was suddenly flowing through me.

The trouble was, it didn't last. Within minutes of leaving I felt as though my head had been cracked in two. The pain made me dizzy and I felt like I was about to fall. I managed to call Aunt Gulshan and ask her to send Emily to get me. The next thing I remember, I was walking toward a bridge that crossed the river that ran through the city. I felt a strong, dark force pulling me toward the edge of the bridge. I knew it was dangerous, but I was powerless to stop myself.

And I could not swim.

Just as I was about to climb up onto the edge of the bridge, I felt a pair of strong hands clamp my shoulders. "Watch where you're going," said a voice, deep and solid and every bit as strong as the hands themselves, hands which easily lifted me from the ground and carried me over to the grass at the side of the bridge. The man placed me down, and though I looked to see who he was, I could see no one around me.

I sat stunned there in the grass until Emily arrived, pushing Aunt Gulshan's empty wheelchair. I tried to explain what had happened on the short walk back home, but I knew I wasn't making any sense.

Gordon phoned to check in on me, and when Aunt Gulshan told him about my strange phone call and my even stranger story about the bridge and the hands, he came straight around. Together with Emily and Aunt Gulshan, he prayed for me. I started crying, then shouting. "Jesus Christ, save me!" I yelled as behind my tightly closed eyes I saw a demonic figure wearing a black mask teasing and taunting me.

"I'm going to kill you, and your Jesus Christ cannot save you," he hissed, his words conjuring the deepest fear within. I could see Jesus too, but he wasn't saying anything. I tried my best to fight the demon off, but he grabbed hold of my hand and pulled me toward him. There was nothing but darkness where he was taking me, and soon I was almost completely covered by it. Only my left hand remained free. "Look, he cannot save you. He is powerless," the dark presence said. "Say that Jesus Christ is not the Son of God."

Warmth started to flood down from my left hand, and I knew that Jesus had grabbed ahold of me. "He's mine now," he said, and in that moment I saw the demon writhe and wither away in front of me.

I had never experienced anything like it before, and have not experienced it since then. But something changed that evening. Something that had been holding me back was broken.

I knew that forgiving those who had hurt me the most was a pivotal moment for me. And it seemed dark spiritual forces knew it too, making a desperate attempt to lay their claim on me once more. It seemed even they knew I was crossing a threshold of refined, mature faith.

I knew now that when Jesus said he would protect me, he meant it.

So when, a few weeks later, Gordon invited me up to the front of the church and placed one hand on my back and another over my hands that were crossed over my chest, I knew without doubt that I was making the best choice I had ever made in my whole life. I came up from the water feeling as though all the dust and blood and fear from Pakistan had been washed away.

That night I had a dream that took me back to my homeland. But unlike all the other dreams that left me sweating and panting and reaching for the light, this one did not deal in fear and death. This dream was soaked in the same kind of light that I had seen and felt whenever Jesus had appeared to me.

I was back on the same side street next to the school where I had been stabbed, only this time there were no knives or *mullahs*, no angry shouts or violent fists. There was just me, standing in the road, feeling the dust between my toes. I was talking about Jesus and in front of me was a crowd of people listening quietly to me. The light was everywhere, saturating the air with peace. I woke up and knew immediately that this dream was different, that what I had seen would one day happen. I would return and tell people all about Jesus, the Son of God who saved me, protected me, and offered the same love and acceptance to other Muslims just like me. I wanted my family to know this God. I wanted my childhood friends, my community, even Yazie and the Wahhabi to know Jesus. How it would change everything!

My "present" had changed so drastically that I'd been wondering what the future held for me. Now I knew.

The dream captivated me and rooted me in hope for things to come. But in the meantime, God was at work in other areas of my life—areas that were perhaps not quite as exciting but just as important.

God was working on my character, challenging me to become

less selfish. Like any seventeen-year-old, I threw myself into the new adventures of independence, forgetting there were responsibilities waiting for me at home. Aunt Gulshan was never anything less than generous with her money and her home, and Emily's love for my aunt extended to me, but they didn't deserve a houseguest who wouldn't pull his weight. I was bringing no money into the home and was costing them plenty, so it was perfectly reasonable for them to expect me to help out with a little housework.

"You want me to do what?" I said to Emily as she stood outside my room one morning, holding out the vacuum cleaner. I had barely woken up and was not at all ready to face this kind of conversation. "I have never done it before."

Emily looked unimpressed.

I wanted to explain to her what being a Sayed meant. Back home I had never in my life been asked to clean anything. I would leave my room in the morning and return later in the day to find that the piles of clothes and papers and whatever else I had left lying around had been all tidied up. I'd never cooked, never worked in the garden, never washed a car or painted a wall. I was a Sayed, and Sayeds simply did not have to do the work of the lower classes.

I thought about all of this, but even as the words flashed through my mind, I knew they would sound out of place here in England. That part of my life was over, and I think I knew it would never return. So, reluctantly, I did as I was asked and tried to push the machine around the house. I was a failure at it and didn't like to be reminded of the fact that Emily's ten-year-old nephew could do a better job than me. I felt humiliated, not so much by the words but by the task itself. Did I really have to give up being a Sayed in order to become a Christian?

As summer ended and autumn began, my life adopted a strange new rhythm. At times I felt confident in this new path I was on. I enrolled in college, got to know other people my own age, and found that apart from a few struggles with the language, I had the potential to be a diligent student. During these weekdays I could remember what it felt like to be making plans for my future, safe in the knowledge that there were good times ahead. On Sundays and at the times when I met with Gordon or Tim, I found that church gave me a sense that I was in the right place, that I was being invited into an even deeper, more satisfying faith in God. Tuesday games of basketball were special too, giving me a buzz of excitement, reminding me what it felt like to belong to a group of friends. But all along I felt an ache inside whenever I thought back to my family. Missing them was painful, and no matter how much there was to focus on in England, thoughts of life in Pakistan always threatened to make me cry.

For Aunt Gulshan, who had never had a child of her own, the responsibility of looking after me must have been immense. For Emily, who cared so deeply about my aunt in her ailing health, my return brought with it extra complications. For all of us, there was no common map for the journey ahead. Aunt Gulshan and Emily expected me to behave like any Pakistani child would: showing them respect, taking care of them, and fulfilling their requests without question. I wanted something else: both to have the freedom that my friends at college had and also not to lose the privileges my birth had given me. We argued more than we should have. Almost every time we did, I dialed the number of my home back in Pakistan, hoping Ami would pick up and I could talk to her about everything. But she never did. The phone just rang and rang.

Months passed and autumn faded into winter. Beneath all the confusion about how I should be treated in the house, there was an obvious cause, but one we rarely spoke of. Though I checked the post carefully every day, I still hadn't heard from the Home Office about my appeal. By the end of December, it had been over nine months since I made my claim for asylum, and though I made repeated calls to my solicitor as well as the Home Office, the only response I ever received was the same old news that they were updating their systems and I would be notified of the decision within six weeks.

Finally, the letter came. I was given a date to return to the office and be informed of their decision. Three weeks later Emily, Natasha, Aunt Gulshan, and I sat in the same large waiting room. It was quieter than I remembered it, though my heart was beating loud enough to drown out most other sounds.

"Ali Husnain?"

I walked over to the desk. A man I didn't recognize sat there.

"Our computers have gone down. We cannot give you a decision today."

I was confused and called Natasha over to make sure I had understood the man correctly.

"But someone must have made a decision already," I said. "Surely someone in this building knows what you are going to say—otherwise, why send the letter inviting me here? Please, can you go and find the person and have them tell me what they decided?"

"I'm sorry," he said in a way that told me he was not at all sorry. "We can't do that. But go home and I promise that you will have a letter from us after the weekend."

Natasha and I retreated and tried to plan another response. We phoned the solicitor, but he said there was nothing we could do but leave and wait a few days for the letter.

I was angry when we got home, slamming doors and refusing to speak.

"Why?" shouted Aunt Gulshan. "Am I not giving you enough here? You've got your room, your computer, your clothes. Is all that not enough? And why do you want to phone home all the time? Is it not enough for me to look after you? Are you wanting to complain to your mother about me?"

I couldn't reply. I didn't want to complain about Aunt Gulshan, and I didn't want to tell her that she was partly right. What she was able to give me was not enough. Having clothes and a room and a computer was fine, but I wanted more. I wanted a job and a bank account and the knowledge that I belonged here. She was powerless to give me any of those.

The weekend came and went and the letter never arrived. A week passed and still no envelope with the Home Office stamp. Though I ran downstairs whenever I heard the post arrive, none of it was ever for me. I phoned my solicitor and complained, and he called me back telling me that whenever he checked he was always told that the letter was on its way. "You're powerless, I'm afraid. There's nothing you can do but wait."

It wasn't until February that I received the letter. It was too thick to post through the door, and the language was too complicated for me to be able to understand every word. But I knew enough to understand the meaning behind it all. I had been refused.

"They don't believe you're telling the truth," said my solicitor when we spoke on the phone that morning. "They think you made most of it up."

I felt deflated, lifeless, bled dry of any sense of happiness or joy I had ever felt.

"What next?"

"Well, you have seventy-two hours to launch an appeal."

"And if I don't?"

"They'll send you home."

All that was good in my life, any contentment or happiness I had secured in my new life in Oxford, was extinguished with those four words. What's worse, I realized I didn't even know what "home" meant anymore.

CHAPTER 15

"I BLAME GOD"

When the Wahhabi stabbed me that afternoon in Pakistan, I hadn't been able to see the blade as it was driven into my side. But tonight, as I held the kitchen knife taut against my skin, I wondered whether I would be able to watch. Would it be too much for me to look as the blade cut through the tender brown skin on the inside of my left wrist?

It was late and the heating in the house had been off for hours. But I was hot with rage. Aunt Gulshan and I had been arguing for at least an hour.

It had started like it always did. I'd been feeling sad about Ami and my family at home and worried about the latest appeal. I'd lost count of the number of times I met with lawyers in the months that passed since my first application was rejected, first with representatives of one legal firm (until they decided that mine was a hopeless case and they were wasting their time on me), then with representatives of another. I'd answered so many questions about the stabbing and the attacks on me that I was starting to question my own version of events. I was getting frustrated at the way I couldn't recall the little details like the exact words that Yazie's cousins had said as they held me down or the precise phrasing the four men had used when they discussed whether to take me back home or hand me over to someone in Multan.

And I'd been feeling frustrated with the way that Aunt Gulshan wanted me to be happy, and angered by the way she described my life back in Pakistan, telling me I was better off here.

"That is not true," I said. "Life is worse here. Worse even than the forest and the shack. I am more of a prisoner here than I ever was there."

As we shouted back and forth, not caring how much noise I made or whether I could be heard outside, I reached for stronger and stronger things to hurl at her. I was angry and frustrated, and when Emily came downstairs, I said more things that I hoped would end the argument, things I regret, things that some part of me hoped would hurt my aunt.

When there were no more words to say, I reached for the kitchen knife. "I'll kill myself then," I said, the blade tight against my skin. Did I really want to? No. But like a bolt of lightning in a storm, cutting myself seemed like the only act with enough force and power to break through to them. It was foolish and dangerous, but I was desperate.

And so there I was, the blade sending little shocks of pain up my arm. Aunt Gulshan stared. I turned my back on her and Emily. I clenched my empty fist tight and tightened my grip on the wooden handle. I pushed. The knife bit in. Once again I felt white fire burst within me. There was more shouting then, a lot more, but the shock of the pain blocked out almost everything. I grabbed a towel and wrapped it around my wrist. I left the kitchen, pushing past my aunt and Emily, not knowing what time it was or what I was going to do once I got outside.

The cold air hit full force as I opened the door, but I didn't want to stop. I carried on walking, my wrist starting to feel heavy. After a few minutes I paused long enough to look at it. The single gash across my wrist stared back at me like an open mouth. Seeing it like that made me worry for the first time about what I had done, and I phoned one of my friends from church.

It was one in the morning. He answered on the fourth ring.

By two o'clock I was in the hospital having stitches put in.

By the time the sun rose I was back home, hoping I could put off the explanation and apology I owed Aunt Gulshan and Emily until the next day.

Even though there was much to enjoy in England, I was bothered by the way my mood fluctuated depending on how the appeal was going. Whenever I met with a lawyer or heard some news that I thought might be positive, I felt great. But if I was left waiting for too long to hear back from someone who I hoped might be able to help my case, or if for any number of reasons I started to doubt that my appeal would be successful, I came crashing down again.

I thought a lot about Ami in those days. Though I wasn't aware of it at the time, I later found out that when Ami was fighting her own court case in the hope of divorcing my father, Aunt Gulshan was her main source of help besides Ami's parents. Aunt Gulshan had given money and support, even though it felt as though we had been rejected by everyone else in the family.

Though I wished I could go back to showing nothing but gratitude and respect for Aunt Gulshan, I knew my new life in England was a world away from my childhood in Pakistan. At college my eyes were opened to a new way of living, and while I disliked seeing people my age swearing at their parents, I found their confidence and sense of freedom appealing. When I spent time with them, I felt as though I finally had some power again. Turning eighteen only added more fuel to that fire, and the more I wanted to assert my independence, the more Aunt Gulshan reminded me just what was expected of a boy my age from Pakistan.

And that was part of the problem. I was beginning to lose hold of my identity as a boy from Pakistan, but I didn't yet have, or even want, an identity as a young English kid. I didn't know where I belonged. But my struggles went beyond that. As well as wondering which culture I belonged to, I was struggling to understand something even more fundamental: Could I really accept that I was a sinner?

A song from church that I liked included the line "I'll never know how much it cost to see my sin upon the cross." Every time I sang it I cried. I felt like I was breaking inside, as if deep cracks were opening up within me. I never thought I had done much wrong in my life, yet in these moments at church I felt consumed by guilt. I knew I had sinned, but how, and what could I do about it?

Growing up as a Muslim, I'd been taught that there were two types of sins: those that could be forgiven and those that could not. I had never committed an unforgivable sin—not until I became a Christian, at least—and so I had learned that most sin was easily dealt with by sacrificing an animal, which we did once a year around Eid. Sometimes extra problems would arise—perhaps something was going wrong with Baba-jan's business or someone in the family was in poor health—and Ami would suggest that we put things right by giving some money to the poor. But these little sacrifices were our attempt to get Allah to bless us, not to confess anything that we had done wrong.

So I had no real concept of sin in the way that Christians understand it. I knew there were times when I did things that were wrong—perhaps lying to a teacher to get out of homework or telling Ami that I encountered a large queue of people when I went out for food but instead had just wanted to spend more time at Uncle Faizal's—but as long as what I was doing made me happy, I could see no harm in it.

Christianity was different. Admitting that I messed up, and that I messed up regularly, was not an easy thing for me to do. I didn't like to see myself that way. I felt weak, naked, and vulnerable, as well as embarrassed and disgusted by the truth about myself.

And yet, that was never the end of the story. Every time I felt the cracks open within me and wept and said I was sorry to God, a sense of peace always followed. Eventually I knew for sure that I had been forgiven. I'd never known anything like it before.

During my second year since escaping Pakistan, there were times when my aunt and I would pray and read the Bible. Sometimes we would stay up late, all night in some cases, praying and reading Scripture. I would feel exhausted the next day, but grateful for the chance to reconnect with my aunt and my faith. I felt close again to my friends at church and spent time with Gordon and Tim, and even accepted Eddie's invitation to join him as he visited cafés along the Cowley Road, talking to Muslims about Jesus. I rarely said anything on those visits—the fear was too strong within me to fully unlock my tongue—but being around someone so free in his faith was almost intoxicating. For days after I could feel the sense of excitement within me.

But however tightly I tried to hold on to these experiences, the unanswered question of my asylum remained. It was like a dark moon, always present in my sky, sometimes full and dominant, sometimes almost hidden. But it was never absent.

My appeal had been rejected two months after I made it, and again I had been told that I had seventy-two hours to leave the country or ask that my case be considered by a higher court. My lawyer bailed at that point, but Natasha managed to persuade him to file the appeal anyway, reminding him that it would take no more than an hour of his time to do so. He agreed and I went back to waiting for the post to deliver the verdict.

It took months for the second rejection from the High Court to come back to me, but in the meantime Natasha found me a husband-and-wife team of lawyers who were also Christians and were happy to take me on. Just like before, I was able to claim legal aid and so get my fees paid, but I also knew that just like with the first lawyer, I would only have one or two shots at it.

The new lawyers were better. Gordon introduced me to an American charity that supported persecuted Christians, and they agreed to vouch for me, acting as expert witnesses in the hope that their opinions might strengthen my appeal.

I hoped they were right, but there were times when I doubted whether anything would work. I wondered whether the best thing for me would be to go back to Pakistan and face whatever fate was waiting for me. I told Gordon this one day, but he just smiled gently. "I blame God," I added, hoping to get a reaction.

"Yes," he said after a long pause. "I know. But you matter, Ali. You belong. You can get a revelation from God just as much as I can."

His words were like clear air after a tunnel that threatened to never end. We prayed and I left with the memory of what it felt like to have hope within me.

Aunt Gulshan was waiting for me when I got home. She looked worried.

"I spoke to your mother," she said. At first the words didn't make sense to me. Almost two years had passed since I had seen or spoken to Ami, and though I had called a hundred times, I'd almost forgotten that it was possible that someone else might still be able to talk to her.

"She said that they moved back to the house recently, but as soon as they did they started to receive threatening phone calls. They have had letters too."

The thought that they had moved back to the house sent my heart in two opposite directions, filling me with joy and at the same time with sorrow. "What did the letters say?"

"They said that if you return, they will kill you and your family. The letters say that there is a *fatwa* against you."

It was nothing new to know that these people believed that I was apostate and wanted me punished by death. But even so, hearing about the *fatwa* instantly canceled out the last tiny hope I'd been nurturing within me from the moment I boarded the flight and left Pakistan. The shock hit me like a gut punch. Finally I knew that I could no longer hope that it was all going to go away. I would never be able to quietly return home and hope that everything had been forgotten.

"That was not all," Aunt Gulshan said. "Your mother said they have to go to court to swear that they no longer consider you their son. If they don't disown you, they'll all be at risk."

Even to this day I believe that those words hurt more than any knife. The ache they unleashed within me was too fierce to do anything else than run upstairs to my room and weep. "Jesus," I prayed once the tears had subsided enough, "is this the way it has to be? Is this the only way to keep my family safe? I need you to protect them as you have protected me. Would you reveal yourself to them just as you have revealed yourself to Aunt Gulshan and me?"

In time Ami emailed me copies of the *fatwa*, the letters that threatened to kill her and the others as well as the legal affidavits that she and Baba-jan signed, publicly disowning me. It was too hard for me to read them, but I knew they would be helpful in my appeal. Between this new evidence, my new lawyers, and the experts from America, I started to hope that finally I might be able to persuade someone to let me stay. And when the day of my court appearance came and I watched the Home Office lawyer arrive looking flustered and confused, my heart started to leap.

"Your Honor," she said once the judge had arrived and we had all taken our seats, "I would like some more time to study this case."

The judge was not pleased, and she told her so. "You have thirty minutes."

We all left the room, and along with Aunt Gulshan, Emily, my two lawyers, and James, the representative from the American charity, I went outside to get a coffee. It felt pretty good, standing there in the early spring sunshine, watching the traffic crawl along the busy town center road, listening to the rest of my team talk excitedly about how unprofessional it was for a lawyer to arrive so unprepared. "This is looking good, isn't it?" I said as we walked back in. Nobody could hide their smile.

Back inside I faced the same questions I had already faced dozens of times. What did I say to Yazie and my friends? How did I get stabbed? How many people attacked me? How many days was I with Hassan? When did I leave Gujranwala, and where did I go next? I listened carefully to the questions as they were repeated by the interpreter and made sure that I was as precise as possible in my answers.

The lawyer who was questioning me was clear about where she

thought I was lying. She referred to the statement given by my aunt and pointed out all the ways in which our two versions of the story did not match. I became a little anxious for a moment, but when we took the next break and Aunt Gulshan left so that she could have her dialysis treatment, everyone told me not to worry. The evidence was in the *fatwa*; she was fighting a losing battle.

The final session was like a boxing match. My lawyer and the Home Office lawyer traded accusations and responses, talking so fast that I struggled to keep up. But I knew what was going on and I could tell when they were talking about the *fatwa* and the affidavit and the threatening letters that my parents had received. I knew the Home Office lawyer didn't believe a word of what I said. I thought maybe if she had read my case properly she would have felt different, so when it came time to leave, I was happy enough to walk over to her, offer my hand and a smile, and say goodbye, just as I had with the judge.

"I think we're going to win this," said my lawyer quietly as we left.

It took weeks to hear from the Home Office, though not nearly as many as before. When Aunt Gulshan phoned me while I was at college to say that a large package had arrived, a part of me was unsurprised when she read to me the final verdict on the final page. "I dismiss the appeal," she read.

I was crushed, and scared as well, but the process was becoming familiar to me and I guessed that I would go through another appeal. It was not ideal, and I was desperate to get a job and a bank account, but the threat of being deported had started to lose its bite.

I phoned my lawyer. "I got the letter," I said. "When are you going to make the appeal?"

She was quiet on the phone. "That's the problem, Ali. We can only appeal if we have new evidence. Without it there's nothing we can do."

"But what about the *fatwa* and the letters and my parents disowning me because they're scared that they might get killed too? That's all new evidence, isn't it?"

"No. That was new for that last appeal, and it got rejected. There's nothing we can do. I'm sorry."

I was walking back from college and called James. It was morning in America, and he answered quickly.

"Leave it with me," he said. "I'll see if we can take it to the European Court."

All these courts and all these lawyers, all these chances to appeal and all these rejections. My head was confused. Where would it end? I couldn't imagine it would ever be possible for me to convince a judge that I was honest, for the harder I tried and the more evidence I had to show them, the more they seemed to distrust me.

I sat down in a bus stop and waited. I thought about God and wondered if I could ask for help. Why was it that I found it easy to pray when I was feeling full of optimism? Even when I was suffocating with fear I had learned to cry out for God's help, but now, when I was feeling as though someone had removed all traces of hope from my life, I had nothing. Why was I mute like this? Why was I numb?

CHAPTER 16

HUNTED DOWN

The only thing that gave my life a sense of normalcy in this dark time was college.

The work was challenging and my English was improving all the time. I never quite understood why it was that English people my own age were happy to leave the house wearing what looked to me like their pajamas, but I was content to add this to the list of Strange Things I Will Never Understand about the English. They take their rabbits to be treated by the vet and use naked women to advertise everything from chocolate to motorbikes, but on the whole I have always found them to be as Aunt Gulshan told me when I first arrived, kind people who treat others fairly.

Even though it sometimes caused Aunt Gulshan to worry about me, I always made my way home slowly from college. It gave me time to think. At college I was a teenager in England, but once I got home I was a Pakistani nephew. Sometimes I found it easy to move between the two worlds, but there were times when I needed more than the walk and the bus journey would allow. On those occasions I would take a walk after we had eaten our evening meal and sit and watch people unwinding in the evening in the local park. I still played basketball with people from church from time to time, but as I entered my thirteenth month of waiting to hear back from the European Court of Human Rights, I had lost my passion for shooting hoops on my own. It all seemed like too much work.

In the year since James had made the appeal, I had been through the usual range of emotions. I'd been desperate and numb, anxious and excited, sad and very sad. But there had been good things about the year as well: I had turned twenty, made good progress in my studies, and, best of all, had started talking on the phone to Ami again. Even though Baba-jan didn't approve and each call was separated by a month or more of silence, our conversations helped. As I listened to her talk about how big Misim was getting and how Zainab was excelling at her studies, I knew I still had a family, even if they had told the courts that they disowned me.

"Misim came back from school yesterday," Ami said toward the end of one of our calls. "He told me that he had been asked by his teacher who his hero was. Everyone else in the class talked about cricketers or movie stars, but Misim told everyone that his hero was you."

These words carried me through for days, like a blood transfusion administered to a terminally ill patient. When their power faded I looked forward to the next call, or to the nights when in my dreams I was at home among my family, not doing anything more exciting than sitting around the lounge, watching the ceiling fans stir up the air. In those dreams everything was normal, everything was fine. When I woke up I could still feel my family close by, as if the air still held their shadows.

I was thinking about one of these dreams as I sat in the park that evening, watching owners play with their dogs. People had been talking all day about how hot it was, and though the sun's heat had been nothing compared to the fierce blaze that baked the earth back home, I was happy enough to close my eyes and feel the last of its warmth for a while. When the sun dipped and the air cooled, it was time to go home.

Aunt Gulshan was looking out the front window as I returned, her hands clasped in front of her mouth. "I had a call," she said as soon as I shut the door behind me. Her breathing was rapid and though her voice was quieter than usual as she repeated those four words, it was obvious that whatever had happened had terrified her.

Eventually I calmed her down enough so she could explain. "There were people shouting. First they said, 'Where is Ali?' I was going to tell them, but then I heard someone in the background shout, *'Allahu akbar!'* and I knew something was wrong. They started saying that you were an infidel and that you deserved to die. They said they will call tomorrow at two and if I don't tell them where you are, they will come and kill us both."

Her words raised an old fear in me, as fresh and toxic as it ever was. I called Tim and Gordon and told them enough for them to come around straightaway. It was only when I heard the sound of their knocking on the door that I realized Aunt Gulshan wasn't the only one who was scared. I imagined the door exploding open and men with knives coming in to kill me, the old familiar band wrapping itself around my chest again, squeezing all the air from my lungs.

We all listened to Aunt Gulshan tell the story again and Gordon phoned the police. Two officers arrived soon after and for the third time I heard my aunt describe the call and the threats and the 2:00 p.m. deadline. Each time I felt worse, and a pain had started up in the place where I'd been stabbed more than three years earlier.

The police, however, were not panicking. "We're going to leave a car outside your house tonight and we will come back tomorrow morning and record the phone call if it comes in." Their calm approach to the situation seemed to imply this kind of thing happened all the time, as if it was all just routine. For me, though, it was worse than any of my nightmares.

Tim and Gordon stayed until late in the night, talking and praying with me long after Aunt Gulshan went to bed. When I was the only one awake in the house, I checked that all the doors were locked, went to my room, and pushed the chair up tight against the handle.

I sat on the floor beneath the window and listened. It was quiet outside, just a few distant passing cars to break the silence. For a moment I was back in the shack in the middle of the forest, desperately trying to separate the usual noises from the ones that might indicate that I was about to be attacked.

I tried closing my eyes, hoping I might be able to sleep through some of the night, but it was impossible. The fear was keeping me awake, though I was tired right down to my bones. I was tired of waiting, of running, of having to rely on people to protect me. And I was tired of the pain that reared itself whenever I thought about Ami, Zainab, and Misim. Saying goodbye at Lahore airport had been agony, but the feelings were even more intense now. If I could have flown back to Pakistan that moment and let the Wahhabi kill me and put an end to it all, I honestly think I would have.

Gordon and Tim arrived early the next day, with two new police officers following later with their recording equipment. We were asked the same questions from the night before, and Aunt Gulshan was given strict instructions to keep the callers on the phone for as long as possible to allow them to trace the call. The minutes moved slowly until 2:00 p.m. The phone remained silent. Nobody moved as we were stuck like statues in the front room while Aunt Gulshan waited by the phone in the hall. I was sure everybody could hear the sound that was filling my own ears as my blood raced around my body.

The sound of the call coming in caught me by surprise. "Hello," said Aunt Gulshan.

The sound of shouting in Urdu filled the front room. *"Allahu akbar! Allahu akbar!* The boy's an infidel and he has brought shame to Muhammad! We will kill him! *Allahu akbar!"*

I watched one of the police officers motion to Aunt Gulshan to try to calm them down, but it was no use and she replied with just as much force, shouting into the phone. "How can you call him an infidel? You're disturbed. It is you who has got their religion all wrong. You're a disgrace."

The phone line went dead.

"What happened?" I asked.

"They hung up," said the officer, looking cross. He was about to say something when the phone rang again. More Urdu filled the room, but there was less shouting this time and Aunt Gulshan, a police officer at her side, kept calm.

"If you know where he is, you should tell us. If you don't, we will come and burn your house down and kill you instead. We don't care about the police. We've got people on the Cowley Road and we will send them around to do it."

I looked at the police officer standing near me, but it was obvious that the Urdu was lost on him. Tim understood, though. He looked pale.

Once the call ended, I tried to translate what they had said. The police left soon after, I guess to check with whoever was tracking the call and to match what Tim and I told them with their own translation of the call. When they did return, they looked serious.

"The call came from Pakistan, but you were right about what they said about the Cowley Road. We know which mosque they mean."

"Why don't you send someone round to question them?" said Gordon.

"We're not going to do that."

"Why?" Gordon asked.

"Because we don't want to inflame the situation. We don't want to trigger a riot here. Our best advice is for you to leave, Ali."

I didn't expect this. "Why can't you protect me here?"

"We don't have the resources. We can't protect you around the clock, but let us find you somewhere else to live and we're confident that they won't be able to find you."

I hated the idea and told them so. "I'm tired of running," I said. They had no reply.

I was only just beginning to feel at home again, and now I was being asked to leave.

For the first few days after the phone calls I held out, telling everyone I was going to stay, but I knew I would have to go eventually.

When a week passed and Gordon sat with me and told me that for my own safety as well as my aunt's I ought to go, I finally agreed.

My one condition when I visited the police was that I wanted to be moved to a Christian family who went to church. If I was going to hide like this, then I knew I would need to be with people who could help me in my faith.

"Okay," said the officer who had introduced herself as Detective Moore. "Tell me all the cities and towns where you have been in the UK. I want to know everywhere you know someone and everywhere you are known."

Three days later I walked back in toward town. The police had given me clear instructions: Don't tell anyone what you're going to do, don't bring too big a bag, don't talk to anyone as you walk. After a mile or two I waited in the pub car park, looking for the gray sedan they told me to expect. Eventually it arrived, and I recognized Detective Moore in the passenger seat. A man was driving. Neither of them wore a uniform.

"We've got a long drive ahead of us," she said.

"Where are we going?"

"I can't tell you. Even Detective O'Shea here doesn't know."

We drove in silence and I was soon asleep. I drifted in and out, waking occasionally to hear Detective Moore give directions or discuss some aspect of the news. Eventually I was awake enough to read a sign that read "Colchester." I knew it was somewhere northeast of London, but we carried on driving, out through the town and down fast roads that cut through open, flat fields.

Eventually I couldn't hold it in any longer. "Where are we?"

"Frinton-on-Sea."

"Where's that?" I had never heard of the place. "Are we still in England?"

Detective O'Shea smiled, and as we slowed and entered a village, I looked at the houses passing by. It was a nice place, quiet and neat with plenty of space between the houses. Seagulls were barking and the sky was clearer than in Oxford. There were no tall buildings and no tall trees. Just a wide sky peppered with clouds.

Detective Moore directed the driver to park down a road that ran alongside a wide-looking house. "Wait here while I go and see whether they are ready for you."

We waited. "Remember," said Detective O'Shea, "they don't know anything about you or where you're from, and they're not allowed to ask. And you can't talk about anything from your past either. Not ever. Do you understand?"

I nodded. Outside my window I could sea the ocean, lying flat and still beyond a bank of grass. I inched my window down and breathed in. I had never smelled the sea before.

Once inside the house, I met Ann and Terry. I liked them right away. She had a way of smiling with her eyes that told me she was kind, and he was tall and gentle and I knew in an instant that I could trust him. But I was tired and struggled to stay awake.

Detective Moore told me before she left that I wasn't to have any contact at all with anyone back in Oxford. That was a hard thing to hear, especially since back in Oxford I'd had to make hasty goodbyes through phone calls to Natasha and Tim, and a brief conversation at home with Gordon. Aunt Gulshan and Emily had been waiting by the front door when I came downstairs on the day I left. All of us were too upset to really say anything.

When I woke up late on the first morning in my new home, I was struck by how alone I felt. The house was unfamiliar; even its smells and sounds made no sense to me. I lay in my bed and wondered whether I had just made a terrible mistake.

Part of me hoped the feelings would go away in time. I'd made a new start for myself in Oxford, so why couldn't I do the same here? But even though Ann and Terry were just as kind and gentle as I'd first imagined them to be, I found myself slipping further and further into sorrow. The words that I had said to the police when they first suggested that I move came back to me again and again: I was tired of running. I had no power left in me.

The mornings were the worst. Regardless of whether my dreams had brought terror or a moment of sweet relief, in the seconds after I awoke, I always went through the same painful process as I remembered what my life was like. It was as if every night a part of my brain tried to forget about the previous three years, and for a few seconds I would awake to feel like a normal Pakistani boy who belonged to a large and loving family. But each morning I had to kill that part of me, and the killing only seemed to get more painful with each day that passed.

Ann and Terry welcomed me into the family. They paid for me to enroll in college, and their act of generosity left me feeling amazed. Despite the good times I spent with them during my first days at their home, there weren't enough of them to outweigh the bad moments I experienced. There were so many more hours each day when I felt sad, so many moments when I felt tired. On more than one occasion, I found myself thinking that if there was a way to trade in my new faith to get my old life back, I would do it in an instant. But I knew it was impossible. I knew I was stuck.

I tried calling Ami, but she and the family were away for the summer and it would be another month before she would be back and able to talk to me via her computer. Even though Detective O'Shea had told me clearly that I was not to make contact with anyone back in Oxford, I started calling Aunt Gulshan. Just hearing her voice was enough to make me feel better, but even that was taken from me when Detective O'Shea phoned me one morning.

"Why have you been calling your aunt, Ali? We told you that it was not safe for either of you to call."

I was upset and the tears flowed. It was hard to get my words out. "What can I do?" I said. "Who can I call?"

She had no answer for me.

Then things got worse. James called with news about the appeal he had made to the European Court of Human Rights. "I'm sorry," he said. "They rejected it."

He went on to talk about how we could appeal and that he would set it in motion right away, but I was barely listening. Sometime, somewhere, they would catch me. I was convinced of it. The Wahhabi would track me down and do to me what they'd been threatening to do since I was almost seventeen years old. And now, at last, I didn't care. I just wanted it to be over. Did I trust Jesus still? Yes. Did I still believe that he spoke the truth when he promised to protect me? Yes. But the part of me that was able to choose to trust God was struggling under the weight of all the fear and weariness. I felt like a worn-out warrior entering his final battle.

I felt overwhelmed by how much I had lost already. I had given up my life of Sayed privilege and entitlement and seen it replaced by the humble servanthood of Christianity. I had said goodbye to my family and like a fugitive had been forced to accept life on the run. I'd given up any claim to hating those who had tried to kill me, offering them forgiveness instead. And I'd lost the sense of knowing that I belonged. At times, the weight of all that loss was almost too much to bear.

Not long after James's call, I had a dream.

I was standing in the small hall where Terry and Ann's church met. The ceiling was lower than usual and the chairs hadn't been put out yet. But I was there, standing in the middle of a tight circle of people. Tim was there, and so was Gordon. Ann and Terry, Natasha, Eddie, my friends I played basketball with back in Oxford. There were others too, people whose names I couldn't recall but whom I knew I loved and trusted. As I stood in the middle, I felt my legs give way and I fell backward. I wondered how much it would hurt when I hit the floor, but instead of hard stone slamming against my bones, I felt strong hands hold me up. I was put back on my feet again. Then my legs crumpled and I fell again, in a different direction this time. Again I didn't hit the ground but instead was caught by my friends. Again and again it happened, and every time I fell, someone was there to catch me.

I woke up. I could tell it was morning, but I wanted to keep my eyes shut for just a while longer, to savor this sense of safety just a bit more. The dream was still real enough for me to sense it, strong enough in my memory for me to replay it. Slowly it faded. I remembered who I was and where I was, but for once it didn't hurt so much.

CHAPTER 17

MORE THAN
I DESERVED

Terry and Ann had taken me along to their church the first weekend I was with them. At the time I wasn't sure it would help much, but I was bored and sad and had nothing better to do, so I joined them as we took the short walk to the church. It was nothing like the other places I'd been to. My church back in Oxford was full of people of all ages, especially students my age, and there was a noise in the room before the service started that reminded me of the excitement in the air at the start of a *majlis*. The same feeling was even stronger at the large meeting in Birmingham that I'd gone to with Aunt Gulshan, and even her own church, though smaller, had the same undercurrent of din and chatter running throughout the service. But Terry and Ann's church was different. The building they met in was small, just a single room really, and each Sunday started with the task of setting out the twenty or thirty chairs required for the congregation.

Terry and Ann's children were grown up and had left home, and they seemed to like having me around the house. Each evening at six I would go downstairs and wash my hands, ready to help Ann as she cooked the main meal. She taught me how to chop and how to mix, and though I struggled with baking and other complicated things, I was pretty good at preparing pasta and sauces.

Between home and church I began to feel as though I belonged, and though I didn't know it at the time, I was making an important shift within. All my life I had been a recipient of religion, more like a *mureed* than a *zakir*, following the rules and regulations as they were laid out for me. I prayed what I'd been taught to pray at the times that I'd been taught. The religion I grew up with instructed me how to wash and stand and clothe myself and eat and so much more besides. Islam taught me how to live, but it failed to teach me how to be alive.

I think I carried with me some of those old attitudes as I attended church in Oxford. I was a passenger waiting for the journey of each church service to begin. I was a spectator waiting to be entertained.

But in the little church with fewer people than I could count in my classes at college, I had to do something different. I had to take part. I had to think for myself and speak up. I had to contribute, not just consume.

It took a long time, and I don't think I would have stuck it out had I not been so desperate. But desperate is exactly what I was. Though I tried to make a few calls back to people in Oxford, the brief conversations I had were never enough. I talked to Ami from time to time, but again the joy I felt at the sound of her voice was often canceled out by the sorrow of having to say goodbye. Once the sorrow and fear and weariness that I felt when I arrived at Terry and Ann's house started to lift, I realized that instead of being trapped in a dead end, I had just one choice in front of me. I could either trust God or not. It was as simple as that.

I needed to learn to trust God in a lot of different areas. From forgiving Yazie and the others who had tried to kill me to letting go of the fear of what might happen to me in the future. Living out this trust in God, of course, was more complicated. I failed just as much as I succeeded. For every walk along the beach when I felt able to believe that God was in the midst of the mess with me, there were moments in my room when I felt as though nothing was ever going to change. But gradually, day by day, prayer by prayer, step by step, the hope that had been fostered by a thousand little answers to prayer, by hundreds of conversations with caring friends where I felt God's smile and love, started to outweigh the despair. I had rarely doubted that God could save me, but it was belief in my own ability to trust and follow him that had taken more time to grow in strength and stature.

Six months after the two detectives drove me east of Oxford, I took an even longer drive west with Terry and Ann, picking Tim up along the way. After five hours we had crossed from one coast of England to the other and arrived in Wales for the latest, and probably last, attempt at an appeal.

"Who's Ali?" I looked up and saw a tall, slim, confident young man striding down the hallway outside the courtroom.

"I am."

He offered his hand. "I'm Andrew, your barrister," he said. "I'm sorry I'm late."

It all felt horribly familiar. In the days leading up to this appeal, I had made secret visits to Oxford to meet with Tim and my lawyer. We had spent hours going over the case, making sure that we were as prepared as we could be. I had started to hope that this might be it, that between all the evidence and all the praying I'd been doing, this appeal might be the one. But judging by the late entrance and the youth of my lawyer, Andrew, I started to have my doubts.

It got worse when he told me why he was late. "I was due to return from skiing last night, but my flight was canceled and I spent the whole night stuck in an airport. It's been a crazy journey, but I'm here now."

Oh no. An unprepared lawyer whose life of wealth and privilege was a million miles away from my own experience. He obviously didn't need whatever fee he was going to collect for spending just one day in court defending me. What did it matter to him if I got to stay in the country or not? Could things get much worse?

I didn't have to wait long for an answer. We were invited into the courtroom and shown to our seats. Like every other appeal and hearing I had attended in the four years since I arrived in England, this one was held in a room not much larger than the average classroom.

Various desks and chairs were scattered around, all in the same heavy wood that reminded me of home. The judge walked in after us. "So," he said to me, peering down as if at a curious insect. "You've come for another bite of the cherry, have you?"

I wasn't entirely sure what he meant, but his tone told me that he had his doubts about me. I looked over to Tim, who had his eyes closed and looked like he was praying. When he opened them and saw me, he gave me the kind of smile that told me I had a lot to pray about.

Unlike all the other times, I decided not to use the interpreter who was sitting on my side of the room. I always spoke Urdu when I was living with Aunt Gulshan, but after six months speaking English at home with Terry and Ann, I was confident that I would be able to explain myself fully and understand any of the questions that were put to me. Besides, I'd heard all the questions many times before.

After the usual interrogation concerning what happened when and who said what, I left the room while the judge heard from Tim. I didn't feel good about the way it was going.

I was invited back in and prepared to face the Home Office lawyer. He was an older man, and I thought he was much more impressive than my guy. "Why did you not try to move around in Pakistan? Why not try to relocate in your own country?"

I explained that I did move around and told him about what happened to Hassan and Nazia. It surprised me how painful it was to remember those days.

"Why did you not change your name and try to start a new life?"

I was just about to answer when the judge spoke. "That is an unfair question. He is a Sayed who comes from a large family with networks all across the country. It would be impossible for him to do as you suggest."

The lawyer changed his line of attack after that, focusing on the fact that the statements I had given over the years didn't all match up. He was particularly interested in the *fatwa*, and I struggled to remember the date when it arrived and whether it came at the same time as the other bits of evidence that Baba-jan had sent. I felt more nervous than I had ever felt, for I knew what was coming. I knew this was where I was about to lose.

"Your Honor," said my lawyer, "of course there are inconsistencies. If this was planned and fabricated, then his recall of the events should be perfect. But it isn't, because it's real. My client was always more concerned with the content of the *fatwa* and the affidavits declaring that his family had disowned him than he was with remembering the precise date, time, and format in which they arrived. Of course he is confused and has used words he wasn't entirely sure of. This is not a charade; this is real."

The hearing lasted three hours, and despite the fact that my lawyer had performed far better than I first anticipated, I was not confident. Having failed so many times before, what chance did I have of succeeding now?

I was about to leave when the judge called me over. "Ali, I promise that I will look at your case and do my best to reach a fair decision."

I didn't know what to say. None of the other judges had spoken to me like this. Some of them were rude; others acted as if they could not see me. But this man was polite and kind. "Thank you," I said.

I was back in Frinton-on-Sea, alone in the house, when the phone rang. A week had passed since I had been to court, and I was expecting the usual months-long wait before I heard the judge's verdict. Even so, I'd jumped every time the phone rang and noticed the way my heart carried on racing long after Terry or Ann had ended their call. As the phone rang that morning, I told myself it was too soon for my lawyer to be phoning with any real news and guessed that even if the call was for me and about my case, it would be to tell me that there had been a problem or they were just phoning to check in and see how I was. Either way, I tried to sound cheerful as I answered.

"Hello," I said.

"Ali," said my lawyer breathlessly, "I've got really good news for you. You've got permission to stay in the UK."

I was stunned. "Thank you," I said quietly. *Thank you,* I prayed.

"We have to wait seventy hours for the Home Office to appeal, but in most cases they don't."

We hung up soon after and I dropped the phone to the bed. The house was silent, but the seagulls were fighting again outside and the cat had taken up its usual position by the window, watching the birds with intent. Four years I had spent hoping for this news, and now that I had it, I didn't know what to do.

I picked up the cat. "I can stay!" I said, sashaying her in front of me in a victory dance. She twisted out of my hands and onto the floor. "I can stay!"

I phoned Ann and told her the news, then Terry, Gordon, Tim, and Aunt Gulshan. With every call I felt the same little burst of excitement, but then a numbness. This was the biggest news of my life, but it didn't feel real.

Eventually I prayed. I thanked God and begged him not to let the Home Office appeal. And when the three days passed and I received the second call from my lawyer telling me that the judge's decision stood, I started to feel a little of the happiness that I had always assumed I would feel.

Even though I hated to leave Oxford, I had come to like living in Frinton-on-Sea. I figured if I stayed there in the little church, if I finished my studies at college and found a job, then I would be on the way to making the kind of life that I wanted. It would be small and it would be quiet, but it would be mine. I would continue to enjoy the welcome of Terry and Ann's family, and I would know that I belonged. Most of all, I would be safe.

Yet Aunt Gulshan was not well. Her kidneys were still struggling to function, and other health problems had started to emerge. Emily told me all this when I phoned one day and added that she was about to go back to India for a few months. Though she didn't ask, I knew I needed to return to Oxford and look after my aunt.

I said goodbye to Terry and Ann but told nobody else about my plans. I was nervous about going back, but if my time in Frinton-on-Sea had taught me anything, it was that my life was better for taking a risk and trusting God. He had told me he would protect me, and he did. He had provided me with far more than I deserved, and I was grateful.

Even so, as I returned to Oxford, the fear came creeping up behind me as before. Would the Wahhabi be able to find me now? Did they know I was back? I stayed away from the Cowley Road and tried my best to avoid having anything to do with people from Pakistan. Yet within a month I was feeling confident enough to stop hiding in Aunt Gulshan's house and make contact with my old friends.

I still had a few more months of study to complete, so I enrolled in college again. This time, however, I didn't feel so much like an outsider. After all, I knew that I belonged. Not living under the threat of deportation was a boost to my confidence, and where I had kept myself apart a little before, I now allowed myself to make friends with people. Plus I had a bank account and a part-time job in a computer store. For the first time in years I was able to go out with my friends and not have to account for every last coin and note that I spent.

Another shift was taking place within me as well. Gradually I was feeling less and less caught between my Pakistani heritage and this new English culture. Perhaps it was because I knew I wouldn't be sent home that I finally chose to abandon my history and become like the English people I saw around me. I started to dress a little more like them, listen to the same music, and learn to appreciate and expect the same freedoms. My life was finally mine and I was determined to make it count.

I wanted to belong and I wanted to be free. I went about it all the wrong way.

I made so many mistakes that I lost count of them all. All those years that I spent waiting for permission to remain in the UK were years when my life existed in a strange kind of bubble. With no job and no bank account, I had no money, so my life was simple. I played a little bit of sport from time to time, and there were periods when I met with lawyers to prepare my case, but these took up only a fraction of my time. Most of my life was spent either at home, at college, or at church. That was all there was to it.

So when I finally was told that I could stay, that I could have a job, put my money in a bank account, and get credit cards, I jumped into my newfound freedom with all the enthusiasm of a kid diving into the deep end on a hot summer day. I made up my mind to enjoy myself, so I did.

There were too many nights when I got drunk, too many days when I stared in horror at my bank balance, and too many Sundays when I decided to skip church. In the same way that Baba-jan believed that being a Sayed meant he didn't have to go to the mosque every week, I started to tell myself that my being a Christian was not conditional on church attendance. Besides, I wasn't even all that sure that the people at church would miss me. Where were their concerned phone calls checking on me now? Did they really accept me, or now that I'd been granted asylum and stopped living from one crisis to another, had they all become bored with me?

It was true that the friends I made at college were different from those I made at church. At college I was surrounded by people from different countries, including another asylum seeker just like me. A lot of them had learned English as a second or third language, and many knew what it was like to feel like an outsider. The people at church, on the other hand, were different. Most were white English who had never met anyone quite like me, and conversations with them at youth group only ever revolved around football and TV. I spent far too long sitting quietly on the side, not knowing what to say.

I had felt lonely for so much of my time in England, worse even than I had when I was in the shack in the forest. And I hated feeling lonely. It was as if the sun itself had shifted a few million miles farther away from the earth. Nothing felt right at times like these, and I could glimpse only pale reflections of my former sense of happiness and peace. So one week I decided to carry on testing the limits of my newfound freedom and take a holiday to Spain with a girl who was a friend from college. It was a mistake from the start, but I was flattered that she wanted to spend time with me. I didn't pause long enough to think about whether the trip was wise—or whether I was living in obedience to the One who had saved me.

I came home sad and depressed. Too late, I knew that my mistakes had led me down paths I really didn't want to travel down. Even Ami had heard that I had been getting drunk, and her reaction helped to bring me to my senses. "Nobody in our family has ever been a drunkard," she told me on the phone one day. "So why are you doing it now?"

Days later I found myself on my knees in prayer, consumed with shame over my sin and the mess I had made of everything.

"Jesus, I know you are real, that you hear me and that you care. I want things to change! I don't want to live like this," I prayed. "But I am powerless. Can you help me, please?"

A few days later I knew I had my answer. "You know, Ali," said Gordon during one of our regular conversations, "there's nothing you could do to make me reject you. And it's the same with God. He's not angry with you."

Gordon's words made me pause. God was not angry with me? That was a strange sentence, the kind I simply couldn't ignore. It was too much to take in, yet I knew I couldn't carry on as before.

I remembered the fear I felt when I went into a mosque. I recalled the processions that I and fellow Shia would make each year to celebrate Muharram, where certain men would whip themselves until their backs ran red with blood. I thought about Baba-jan's silence on those endless car journeys where the fear crouched tight in my chest. I thought about the times I'd gotten drunk and shouted in the street until my friends had calmed me down and walked me home. God wasn't angry with me? I had a lifetime of evidence to suggest otherwise.

After all, I was never a good Muslim. And now that Jesus had given me everything, I knew that I wasn't a good Christian. The guilt weighed heavy upon me, though I continued to trip up. It was a miserable cycle.

And yet something about Gordon's words rang true. I remembered Aunt Gulshan's tender prayers as I lay on the *charpai* with my leg red hot with pain. I saw Ami's tears as she said goodbye. I thought back to my dreams and visions of Jesus, so bright with light, so rich in love. Putting out the chairs at church with Terry and Ann, the judge's kind face at the end of my appeal, and a thousand other memories of kindness from Gordon, Tim, and so many others.

God was not angry with me.

It was a mantra I had never heard before, one that felt strange on my lips. But once I said them I knew that these were words that I wanted to say over and over.

"Of course the really important question you need to ask yourself," said Gordon, pulling me out of my daydream, "is this: If it's not anger that God feels toward you, what is it that he feels instead?"

CHAPTER 18

REPAYING HATRED WITH LOVE

It struck me there, on the floor of Gordon's office, with tears on my cheeks and heavy breaths weighing down my chest, that I had made my life busy with all these new distractions of socializing, spending and earning money, and getting myself in and out of little crises. Somehow I had squeezed God out. At least when I lived in the bubble, I had plenty of time to pray, think, and talk about God. This new life I had created for myself looked as though it was full of freedom, but now I realized I'd just ended up getting trapped in my own mistakes.

Eventually it dawned on me that trying to live two lives is just about the hardest thing a person can do. Tim was the one who helped me to see this for myself. I can still remember the day the scales fell from my eyes. It was one of those dry, cold winter days when the sun shines bright and every blade of grass, every tree, and every lamppost looks as though it could snap in two if only you grabbed it just right. We were walking by the river, watching the ducks and swans fight over bread that was being thrown at them by an old man on a bench. We were talking about Tim's work researching Muslims who convert to Christianity, and he was telling me about something he called the "search for identity."

"For a lot of people the search really kicks in once they've decided to become a Christian. That's when all sorts of questions come up: Which community do you belong to now? Who are you going to marry? What's your lifestyle going to look like? Who are your role models? They're all important questions, but answering each of them takes time.

"Then there's another search that people who are immigrants experience. If you're a teenager when you come from Pakistan and then spend several years as an asylum seeker—living as a nobody, someone who doesn't belong anywhere—when you finally do get told that you belong and that you can stay, you've got to work out how to deal with all this freedom. Are you really British, or can you still call yourself Pakistani? Where do you really belong? If you embrace Britishness, are you betraying your heritage?

"Both those searches are hard and they can take years. And for someone like you, Ali, you've got both of them going on at the same time. You're trying to find two new identities. You've got a double struggle within you, and that's hard."

His words sank deep.

He was right. I had been struggling for years. At first it was deciding whether to follow Jesus, but even once I turned my back on my Muslim faith and became a Christian, I found other questions to wrestle with: Could I forgive others? Could I accept that I needed to be forgiven? Would I trust God or try to take control of my life for myself? The answers didn't come quickly. Over time, however, through failure and success, I learned that I could put the pain of the past behind me. It wasn't easy, but I knew that holding on to bitterness and fear would only cause me harm. God held my past, my present, and my future in his hands. I had to let it all go and trust him.

Even once I stopped the drinking and the clubbing and the unwise holidays alone with girls, I still struggled to find my place. I felt hurt by the fact that for a time I was a person of interest in my church, and people would gather around me on Sundays to hear the latest update on my exciting battle to remain in the country. But once it was all done, I felt the spotlight shift away from me. The only thing worse than this kind of rejection was the realization that I'd needed their attention so much in the first place.

Then there was the issue of excitement. In my first year or two of life in Oxford, I'd felt so excited by my faith. But that changed and I went through long periods when I felt that God was distant and unreachable. Feeling this way made me angry at times, for I didn't like how the vitality of my faith seemed to depend on my feelings.

In time, I learned the truth that my feelings matter less than I thought they did and that I can cope with times when God seems a little more distant. But I also learned that when I do feel lonely and discouraged, the best thing I can do is remember all the things God has done for me and pray.

I considered all these things as we walked along the water's edge. Tim said, "You're not alone, though. There are a lot of other people facing the same struggles."

For such a long time I had almost forgotten the dream that came to me the night I was baptized. When my life was overshadowed by lawyers and courtrooms, by fear, anxiety, and sorrow for all I had lost, the dream I had the night of my baptism was remote. In the midst of all my fear and mistakes, I found it hard to believe I might one day be strong enough in my faith to return to Pakistan and preach the good news of Jesus.

But that conversation with Tim was a turning point for me, and about a year after I had returned to Oxford to build a new life for myself, the dream started to come back to me. Sometimes I would dream it again at night, but other times I would replay bits and pieces of it during the day, trying it on again like a favorite old coat brought out from the back of the wardrobe at the start of winter. I loved to remember the feeling of the dust between my toes as I stood in front of the crowd and told them about Jesus. I felt alive as I remembered the faces turned to me, not looking angry or offended, but eager to hear more. And the more I reflected on the dream, the stronger it grew within me. I began to wonder whether there might be a day when I started preaching about God to Muslims like I once was.

I had been on the run for so long, full of fear and anxious for asylum. But I began to wonder if there was some other purpose for my life. And this dream seemed to be at the center.

When I was first in Oxford, I had followed my friend Eddie as he visited the cafés up and down the Cowley Road. He did it so often that he had friends all over the street and would sit for hours talking with different people, most of them Muslims, about God and what it meant to follow Jesus.

When I joined him, I stayed pretty quiet. In those days I didn't know enough about what it meant to follow Christ to be able to really talk about it, and my whole messed-up life was a reminder of what had happened to me the last time I spoke publicly about Jesus. But something was different as I settled into life in Oxford for a second time. It wasn't that I was any less scared, but I noticed that the fear was no longer enough to clamp my mouth shut. Yes, I felt apprehensive, but that wasn't the end of the story. In fact, it was just the beginning.

So I prayed. I watched the news, noticing especially the increase in stories about violence and conflict between Muslims and Christians, and I felt convicted that if ever there was a time for a former Muslim to tell others about Jesus, it was now.

I kept clear of the Cowley Road, but as I walked and prayed elsewhere around the city center, I got talking to people. I met Samir, a Kurdish asylum seeker who hadn't seen his family for seven years, and Abubakr, a man from Pakistan who told me during our second meeting that yes, he would like to read the Urdu Bible with me.

When you find the thing that you were created to do, people say it is as natural as breathing. Week by week, conversation by conversation, I began to notice a change in me. I started to see that talking about Jesus to people who followed Allah was not only easy for me, but it also filled me with a sense that I was doing precisely what God had called me to do. And the more I marched on in that direction, my face fixed toward God, the less I felt the grip of fear.

Of course, though I would like to think my search for identity is all wrapped up, I know I still have far to travel. But even though I am a work in progress, I know God can use me all the same. And as I take each step, as I lay each brick, I know that learning from the people God has put around me is key for me to keep going in the right direction.

"I think that one day I might be ready to leave Oxford," I told Tim one day when we took one of our regular walks along the river's edge. I had just handed in my notice at work at the computer shop and was looking for another job.

"What are you going to do?" he asked.

I paused, though I was not searching for the words. I knew my answer to this question. I had known for some time. But speaking it out loud felt significant—and once the words were spoken, there would be no turning back. "I think God's calling me to be an evangelist. I want to return home one day and preach the gospel among the very people who tried to kill me."

"Like in your dream? The one where you're preaching in the street where you were stabbed?"

"Yes. I think that dream was a gift." Tim looked at me. It was hard to tell what he thought. Did he think I was courageous? Or simply crazy? I carried on all the same. "I know it's a risk, but I think if I can offer them something that will help them physically as well as spiritually, there will be enough support from the Sunni and Shia that the Wahhabi will think twice about trying to kill me."

"Go on," said Tim. We had stopped walking by now and stood facing the water as ducks and rowers floated by.

"I want to tell my story and tell people how God saved me. And just like Aunt Gulshan, I want to travel around from church to church, telling people about my story and raising money. When I have enough, I will return home to Pakistan and build a medical facility that will offer to treat the poor free of charge. And when people ask me why I do this, I will tell them that I am doing it to show that they do not need to be afraid of Christians. I will tell them that I am among them because Jesus taught us to love our enemies. I will tell them that I want to give more love back to my city. They may have hurt me, but I will return with more love. Isn't that what the Bible is all about? Giving love to those who don't even know that they need it? Jesus taught me that."

I remembered Jesus' words to me when I was sixteen, lying on a hospital bed with the stab wound that should have cost me my life: "My son, your life is in danger because of me. You will not die now—I will give you more life."

That day, that dream—it all seemed like a lifetime ago. And yet, as I spoke with Tim, I had the sense that my journey with Jesus was only beginning. He had given me more life. He had freed me from fear of Allah and replaced it with peace in God himself. And now I would dedicate my life to telling Muslims they could have the same.

Tim stayed silent for a long time. He didn't need to say anything. My breath felt like light within my lungs, my heart and head seeming to pulse together in quick time. I knew without doubt that the words I had just spoken would one day come true. It was God's will. Of that I was sure.